THE
ELDER
AND HIS WORK

THE ELDER

AND HIS WORK

DAVID DICKSON

EDITED BY GEORGE KENNEDY MCFARLAND
AND PHILIP GRAHAM RYKEN

PUBLISHING
P.O. BOX 817 • PHILLIPSBURG • NEW JERSEY 08865-0817

Page design and composition by Lakeside Design Plus

Printed in the United States of America

Dickson, David, 1821–1885.
 The elder and his work / David Dickson ; edited by George
Kennedy McFarland and Philip Graham Ryken.
  p. cm.
 Includes bibliographical references.
 ISBN 0-87552-886-4 (paper)
 1. Elders (Church officers) 2. Presbyterian Church—Discipline.
3. Presbyterian Church—Government. I. McFarland, George
Kennedy, 1950– II. Ryken, Philip Graham, 1966– III. Title.

BX9195.D53 2004
253—dc22

2004044154

To the teaching and ruling elders
of Tenth Presbyterian Church,
past, present, and future

and

To Jesus Christ,
the Pastor and Elder of our souls

*If anyone aspires to the office of overseer,
he desires a noble task*

1 TIMOTHY 3:1

*Shepherd the flock of God that is among you,
exercising oversight*

1 PETER 5:2

CONTENTS

INTRODUCTION

Together we serve as elders of Tenth Presbyterian Church in Philadelphia, Pennsylvania. One of us is a ruling elder, the other a teaching elder. People sometimes ask what we enjoy most about the work that God has called us to do in the church, as well as what we find most difficult. Those who ask usually assume that our ministry is challenging. Sometimes they wonder how we persevere through the seemingly endless responsibilities (which in the case of a ruling elder do not even have the benefit of financial compensation).

Our response is that serving as elders in the church of Jesus Christ is one of our highest callings and greatest privileges. One special joy is the fellowship we share with other godly teaching and ruling elders who have the same calling. We belong to a holy brotherhood of elders. Of course our work includes difficult and even discouraging duties, which at times make us wonder why we were ever called to serve. Nevertheless, we believe that what the Bible says is true: the work of the elder is a "noble task" (1 Tim. 3:1).

The noble task of eldership is the subject of this book, which is a short, complete manual describing the personal qualifications and practical duties of elders, especially ruling elders. David Dickson's *The Elder and His Work* was originally printed in Scotland, where it went through more than a dozen editions. The first American edition was published in 1883 in

Philadelphia, a traditional bastion of Presbyterianism. The present text is based on a more recent edition (Presbyterian Heritage Society, 1990) that made use of both of the older Scottish and American editions. Here it has been edited to include Scripture references, to conform to more contemporary spelling and English usage, to offer explanatory notes, and to provide study questions for personal reflection and group discussion.

The Elder and His Work is a useful resource for elder training. Indeed, both of us wish that we had been introduced to this book before becoming elders. Nevertheless, it is equally valuable for seasoned teaching and ruling elders and their wives. It contains many truths of perennial significance for elders, such as the holiness and compassion required for effective spiritual care, the crucial importance of knowing and loving the flock, and the desperate need for dependence on the Holy Spirit to do the real work of the ministry. The book also touches on matters of perennial difficulty for elders, such as balancing the competing demands of home, work, and ministry; speaking with people about spiritual things; dealing with problems in the church; and motivating people to become active in Christian service.

Dickson's approach is thoroughly biblical and pervasively practical. His principles are clearly drawn from the New Testament, especially Paul's instructions to Timothy. At the same time, Dickson shares how he applied these principles in nineteenth-century Scotland. An elder, Dickson says, is a shepherd of Christ's flock and a student of God's Word—a man growing in the gracious disciplines of the Christian life. His account of the elder's work is lively and engaging, and in addition to offering practical advice, he conveys something of the gravity and importance of the elder's calling as a servant in the church of Jesus Christ.

Dickson's practical approach is urgently needed in the contemporary church, where the values of secular culture constantly encroach on church life. *The Elder and His Work* is a beacon of light guiding us back to the Scriptures and illuminating the biblical pattern for leadership in the church. It is also an antidote to the poison of worldliness. Over against the prevailing anti-authoritarianism, philosophical relativism, and self-absorbed narcissism of our day, Dickson advances the biblical ideal of the resolute, strong-minded, and selfless elder—a man after God's own heart. On the solid ground of Scripture, he maintains that God has ordained spiritual authority in the church, specifically in the form of a plurality of elders. In order to preserve and promote his truth in the world, God has given the church courageous, compassionate men who do not live for themselves but for others, caring for spiritual needs by the mercy and grace of Jesus Christ.

David Dickson and His Context

By all accounts, David Dickson was a model elder. He was born in Scotland, the traditional home of Presbyterianism, which simply means spiritual rule by a brotherhood of elders. To be specific, Dickson was born in Edinburgh in 1821. At an early age he entered his father's trade as a wholesale stationer and distinguished himself as an industrious, reliable, and efficient laborer. By age 31 he was considered so trustworthy that he was elected to the town council and soon became city treasurer. Later Dickson became master of the Merchant Company, a professional guild. He also served as one of the first members of the Edinburgh School Board, and at his funeral in 1885 he was honored for his many kindnesses to teachers in the city schools.

Dickson always had a heart for the church, where he labored as a faithful servant of Christ. Ordained as an elder in the Free New North Church at only 30, he served untiringly as clerk of session for 33 years. His handwritten minutes included painstaking records of membership changes and the other spiritual business of the session. But his real passion was always the care of souls, and in this he excelled.

Throughout his tenure as elder, Dickson maintained regular contact with his parishioners, visiting church members in their homes every Sunday evening. Offering words of comfort, a few verses from Scripture, and a prayer for God's help, Dickson was known throughout Edinburgh as a devoted friend and caring Christian gentleman. His selflessness, gentleness, thoughtfulness, and responsiveness to needs in his community marked his life as a churchman. A nineteenth-century biographer provides the following portrait of David Dickson as a worthy elder:

> At the meetings of Session, his genial temper, his strong good sense, his business habits, and his familiarity with the law and practice of the church made him a model clerk.
>
> But it was in his relations to the congregation generally, and to the members residing in his own district in particular, that his value as an elder most strikingly appeared. He was always ready with a warm welcome to every new member, and had a kind word even for the stranger who might turn aside to worship in the New North for a single day. His presence at both services on Sabbath could be confidently reckoned on; and those who

attended the prayer meeting will not soon forget the simplicity, the directness, and the fervor of his prayers.

To the families residing in the district more specially committed to his care, he was indeed a friend and father. He visited them with the greatest regularity, and however short the visit might be, it was never formal. There would always be at least a word of kindly encouragement or wise counsel, and perhaps a pithy anecdote to drive it home. He was particularly fond of children, having wonderfully retained his own youthful vivacity under the pressure of the cares of a very busy life. The natural result was that he was a great favorite with the young, and exercised a very powerful influence over them, which he was always careful to employ in the interest of his Lord and Master. He had a very tender, sympathizing heart, so that he was a frequent and welcome visitor at the bedsides of the sick; and then he was such a bright, happy Christian that his entrance was like a gleam of sunshine in the darkened chamber.[1]

Beyond these personal biographical details, the context of Dickson's career should also be considered. The Industrial Revolution had its early beginnings in the textile factories of England in the middle of the eighteenth century. A hundred years later, industrialization had spread to major urban areas throughout Great Britain. The abundance of manual work in factories was a major cause for families to move to the city. Technological achievements in both agriculture and industry meant that fewer people were required to produce food

1. R. G. Balfour, "Introduction" to David Dickson, *The Elder and His Work* (Dallas, Tex.: Presbyterian Heritage Publications, 1990), vii–viii.

supplies, and this spurred migration into the cities. Throughout the nineteenth century, cities in Great Britain were growing rapidly, often doubling in population in the course of a decade.[2] Industrialization also meant, however, that a significant portion of the population that moved into the cities failed to find employment. Housing, water, sewers, and lighting were poor. Prostitution, poverty, theft, crime, and debt were rampant in urban areas, something not experienced on the same level in pre-industrial Britain.

It was in this environment that David Dickson served Christ as an elder in the church. With so many needs around him, even his customary workload of ten to twelve hours a day did not deter him from ministering to his city district. He viewed his service as an elder as his second vocation—a significant part of his life's work. Eventually his practical experiences as an elder led him to publish *The Elder and His Work*, which is a call to arms for ruling elders to rise up and fulfill the duties they were ordained to perform. No doubt Dickson had observed the failure of some elders to attend to the needs of their congregations. He recounts his experiences to help fellow elders—past and present—understand the essential tasks they have vowed to fulfill.

THE WORK OF THE ELDER

In describing the work of the elder, Dickson moves from the general to the specific. Early sections of the book note the importance, qualifications, and duties of the elder; later sections explain how these duties are to be performed. Through-

2. See Donald Kagan, Steven Ozment, and Frank Turner, *The Western Heritage Since 1300* (Upper Saddle River, N.J.: Prentice Hall, 1998), 762–63.

out, Dickson seeks to provide elders with a ready-to-use manual for their task. His greatest concern was for fellow ruling elders to do their work in a godly and systematic way. He wanted to help them to—as one of his contemporaries aptly put it—"take trouble about things."

Although the Bible provides general guidelines for elders, it does not dictate all the duties of the office. To some extent, the work is undefined, and thus it needs to take shape in the life of an individual elder within his own particular church. As Dickson states, "there is no prescribed or understood plan laid down for him." There is no set hour of the day or time of the week for the elder to do his work. Instead, the elder is to be ready "in season and out of season" (2 Tim. 4:2) and must manage his schedule to make room for the Lord's work. A properly Presbyterian church structure is necessary. Spiritual work is not left to the minister alone, but ruling elders are ordained to serve with him as shepherds of God's flock. An elder who does good work in his assigned area brings glory to God and is a blessing to his people.

The primary work of the elder is spiritual. It was said of the eighteenth-century evangelist George Whitefield that he counted it his first business to be a Christian. This is the first business of any teaching or ruling elder. Through Bible reading, meditation, and prayer, an elder must nurture his own personal relationship with Christ. If he is married, he must also nurture his family by leading in household worship, caring for his wife with sacrificial love, and raising his children with patient affection. Then he must be doctrinally sound. To this end, he must develop his theological acumen by reading, studying, and meditating on the Holy Scriptures, and also by reading theology systematically. He must check to see that what he is taught is faithful to God's Word. But he must also practice what he is learning. Teaching elders must look into the mirror of their own sermons; the lives of ruling elders must reflect the preaching they hear. A good elder is always growing into the image of his Savior.

The elder's noble task demands service to others. In Dickson's case, this meant doing his duty for the people in a specific geographical area. By maintaining a regular pattern of visitation, he was able to meet a wide variety of spiritual needs. Some parishioners needed a word of encouragement, others a word of admonition or correction. Children needed to be catechized. New believers needed to be discipled in the Christian faith. And everyone needed to be "stirred up to pray." In addition to making his regular Sunday-evening rounds, Dickson made unplanned visits to the widows and the fatherless, and to the poor, the sick, and the dying. Based on his extensive experience in visitation, he advises that the elder's conversation must focus on God's Word, first and foremost. Other talk may be appropriate, but the elder must always remember the main reason he is meeting with God's people.

As useful as it is, there are points at which Dickson's description of the elder's work would benefit from further discussion and elaboration. For instance, he spends only a few pages discussing church discipline—a vital and perpetual aspect of pastoral work. Perhaps he had but few examples from which to draw, although it seems unlikely that a growing church in an industrialized city would be exempt from the need for church discipline. In any case, it would help his readers to know more about the proper exercise of church discipline, as well as practical ways to restore individuals to fellowship afterwards. It would also be helpful to know still more about Dickson's practice of pastoral visitation. How did he handle resistance to his ministry? What Scripture did he apply to various spiritual needs? No doubt Dickson had much more to say about these and many other topics. But one of the book's virtues is its brevity, and we may be grateful for the rich legacy Dickson has left for the church in *The Elder and His Work*.

APPLYING *THE ELDER AND HIS WORK* IN THE TWENTY-FIRST CENTURY

The need for the kind of eldership that Dickson advocates is urgent. In its presently weakened condition, the church is desperate for godly men who have the courage and wisdom to defend sound doctrine, as well as the compassion and skill to heal wounded souls. At the same time, tremendous cultural pressures tempt elders to neglect their duties. Even in the church, many people do not want anyone else to be involved in their lives. But if we understand what God requires in his church, we will say today what David Dickson said more than a century ago: "We need no new machinery in the Christian church. It is all provided ready to our hand in the Presbyterian system."

The application of biblical principles in the nineteenth century does not always correspond to the demands of the twenty-first century. How, then, can we best use *The Elder and His Work?* First, the book reminds us that the elder's work is spiritual. His office is not an honorary function; rather, it is a call to spiritual labor. The task demands sacrifice, perseverance, commitment, and sometimes even suffering for the cause of Christ. It requires extra time in studying and meditating on God's Word, in listening to people and their problems, and in counseling and discipling God's people. There is no instant solution for most of the troubles that Christians face. Thus the elder's ministry proceeds "line upon line" and "precept upon precept" (Isa. 28:10). In this respect, the work of the elder has not changed since the nineteenth century, or even since the first century. Elders are still called to care for people's souls.

Second, Dickson's manual suggests many practical ways in which an elder may invest his life in service to God. Even if they are not always directly applicable, many of his ideas can easily be adapted to fit the twenty-first-century context. For example, Dickson advocates personal visitation with members of the congregation. In his context, the best way to accomplish this goal was by spending Sunday evening visiting parishioners in their homes. This may still be practicable in some communities, but in many churches it may not be welcomed, or even feasible. Yet personal contact need not always come through home visitation. What is vital is direct communication. Today some spiritual care can be maintained by e-mail, by talking over the telephone, or by meeting for coffee. The common failure of elders today is not that they use the wrong methods, but that they fail to make much contact at all.

Dickson also reminds elders to be diligent in prayer. The elder should pray faithfully for himself, his family, and his community, and he needs to set aside regular times of prayer for this purpose. But he should also pray for the sheep of his fold and for his minister, keeping a journal of prayer requests so that he will not forget. Elders should also encourage others to pray. One Presbyterian minister recently reported that he had few results from home visits. Schedule conflicts and people's busy lives often limited the spiritual usefulness of visitation. Instead, he opened the church for prayer early

Tuesday and Thursday mornings. The elders would meet to pray for benevolence needs, for the ministry of the church, and for personal requests from the congregation. On occasion, members would call the church during this time to make a request because they knew the elders were meeting for prayer. On special occasions, such as when the prayer time coincided with a national or international day of prayer, the congregation joined the session to pray for wider concerns.

The point is that elders must be men of prayer, praying with and for their people. Whenever a parishioner requests prayer, elders should begin to pray right away: over the telephone, at the computer, during fellowship time after church—whenever and wherever the request is shared. In the twenty-first century, we have communication methods that David Dickson could hardly have imagined (such as e-mail and voice mail), and these are often a help to ministry. Yet there is still no substitute for direct interpersonal contact, with all the warmth of human fellowship that it brings. Whenever possible, elders should meet with people and pray for them in person.

Though vital, prayer is not the only way for elders to shepherd God's flock. To address the pastoral concerns of God's people, a well-organized structure for spiritual care is needed. Dickson's frame of reference was his district—a clearly defined city neighborhood. But the important thing is for elders to have clearly defined duties. Some elders have special gifts for spiritual care and should spend their time doing personal work. Others have spiritual gifts for leadership and should focus their energies on missions, mercy ministry, student work, or some other aspect of ministry. As Dickson put it, some elders should be "appointed to *duties* instead of *districts*."

There are many ways to apply these principles today. One model is the parish system that we use at Tenth Presbyterian

Church, which is located in Center City Philadelphia and includes a widespread membership from New Jersey, Delaware, and the greater Philadelphia suburbs, as well as from the city itself. Some of our elders provide leadership for our Church Planting Commission, Family Commission, Missions Commission, or some other churchwide area of ministry. But other elders have primary spiritual responsibility for the church members who live in a particular part of the city. These "parish elders," as we call them, oversee six parish councils, each consisting of a parish elder plus other active and inactive elders who live in the parish, deacons, deaconesses (nonordained), and a Bible study coordinator. The parish elder directs parish council meetings where the spiritual and practical needs of parish members are discussed. Important concerns from the parish (such as new members, ministry opportunities, or acute pastoral needs) are communicated to the parish elder from the church staff, and vice versa. Work within the parish is thus distributed among the members of the council; other members of the parish are also invited to share the workload. Some parishes also have parish assistants—nonordained men who are prospective officers and have the gifts to help the parish in practical and spiritual ways.

In addition to caring for individual needs, the parish council promotes Christian fellowship within the parish. Some parishes communicate regularly with their members by means of a weekly e-mail newsletter. All of them host social events, which, in addition to parish small-group Bible studies, help church members within a given geographical area get to know one another. The parish model works well at Tenth, but of course would not work in all settings. In smaller churches it might be possible for the pastor and elders to work together even more closely. What is crucial is for elders to exercise spiritual oversight of the people in their congregation, being sensitive to the special needs of the people most directly under their spiritual care. To that end, every session needs to develop and implement a workable plan for shepherding its congregation. In order for people to receive the spiritual care they need, the pastoral burden must be shared in a systematic way.

Finally, Dickson's work is significant for our times because it reminds elders to shepherd the whole flock of Christ. People from all socioeconomic levels and in all walks of life need spiritual care. One noteworthy feature of Dickson's book is how contemporary his ministry agenda often sounds. Like many elders today, he wanted to make sure that rich and poor, young and old, men and women, families and singles, and students and workers all received the pastoral oversight they needed. To that end, he recommended ministry strategies virtually identical to the small groups and targeted ministries that are so common in our day. He also recognized the value of actively employing the spiritual gifts of women and understood the special attention that Christians should give to sharing the gospel with people who don't know Christ, both locally and globally. In many respects, Dickson seems ahead of his time.

One of his special concerns was the spiritual interest that elders should take in covenant children. Today we need to meet young people where they are: performing at school, competing in athletic events, going on mission trips, and participating in social activities. Elders can also develop relationships with children at church by teaching or assisting in Sunday school, hearing children say Bible verses and other memory work, or simply visiting with them before and after church. Elders are called to pay special attention to orphans, showing fatherly concern for those who have lost their fathers through death or desertion. A good elder has a comprehensive concern for the whole flock that is under his care, from the greatest to the least.

We praise God for his faithfulness in giving elders to the church. People can know what it means to live under God's authority only if they have faithful and diligent leaders. God's design is for godly elders to lead by serving the church and its surrounding culture. Our churches, our cities, our nation, and our world will be blessed when God's directives for eldership are understood and applied. David Dickson rightly believed that the noble work of the elder—properly carried out—would lead to the renewal of the church and the reformation of the culture. Our prayer is that this book will challenge, encourage, and instruct a new generation of elders to pursue the good of the church and to promote the glory of God in the world.

George Kennedy McFarland, Ruling Elder
Philip Graham Ryken, Teaching Elder
Tenth Presbyterian Church
Philadelphia, Pennsylvania

1

IMPORTANCE OF THE ELDERSHIP

A pious and useful rector in England once asked me, "What objections have you Presbyterians to bishops?" "We have no objections at all," was my reply; "on the contrary, we have in the Free Church alone 950 of them; but they are bishops of the same order as those ordained by Timothy, and doing the same work, laboring in word and doctrine."

And we might have increased the good man's astonishment still more if we had given him the total number of the *bishops* or *elders*, for the words are used in Scripture to denote the same office. There is only one distinction—that between the elders who labor in word and doctrine (the pastors of flocks) and what are called lay elders, who rule. Besides the pastors, we have in the Presbyterian Churches of Scotland more than fourteen thousand men ordained as elders, to watch for souls as those "that must give account" (Heb. 13:17) and to whom are addressed the solemn words first spoken to the elders of the church of Ephesus: "Take heed therefore unto yourselves, and to all the flock, over which the Holy

23

Ghost hath made you overseers, to feed the church of God, which he hath purchased with his own blood" (Acts 20:28).

What a noble army for the Prince of Peace, in Scotland alone! If all these elders used their office well, what a network of Christian influence would be woven around all our families! What a harvest of blessing in every generation would be gathered in from our beloved land!

I have a deep conviction that, though the scriptural standing of the ruling eldership has been always maintained and defended by Presbyterian churches, it has never been worked out in practice so as to do the good it might do.

The times of the first and second Reformation[1] produced many illustrious elders—men of renown, who did exploits and left their mark on the history of Scotland—yet, in regard to the great mass of them, we cannot find much evidence of minute and systematic work, except as to discipline and the care of the poor. Moderatism[2] did its best to degrade the office by confounding the functions with those of the deaconship—distributing the communion elements and standing at the plate at the church door (*the bawbee elder*)[3] being then con-

---

1. Although the spirit of reformation was introduced in Scotland long before, the Scottish Reformation may be dated to 1560, when the Reformation Parliament repudiated papal authority, severed Scotland's connection to the Roman Catholic Church, and approved the Scots Confession drawn up by John Knox and others. During the so-called Second Reformation (1638–1660), the Reformed and Presbyterian theology and church government of the Westminster Assembly (1643–1648) dominated Scotland's ecclesiastical landscape.

2. Moderatism denotes a theologically more liberal attitude that divided the Church of Scotland in the eighteenth and nineteenth centuries.

3. According to the *Oxford English Dictionary* (Oxford University Press, 1933), a *bawbee* is "a Scotch coin of base silver." So-called bawbee elders did little more than serve communion and collect the offering.

sidered as much as could reasonably be expected of men who had solemnly undertaken a spiritual office! A careless ministry made a careless eldership. In many parishes there were no elders at all in those days; and if the office had not been essential for a seat in the General Assembly, it might have become nearly extinct in the Church of Scotland altogether.

It was no doubt maintained in considerable efficiency in the various Secession churches,[4] as may be seen from Ralph Erskine's *Questions Put to Elders*,[5] and in not a few congregations of the Church of Scotland in the days of Donaldson of Dalgety,[6] Willison,[7] Boston,[8] and others; yet neither in this country nor in America does it appear to have been used as a help to spiritual life in the way of evangelization and edification to anything like the extent to which it is so well fitted to be.

4. The Secession churches included the congregations that for reasons of church polity seceded from the Church of Scotland in 1733 to form the Associate Presbytery and in 1761 to form the Relief Presbytery.

5. Ralph Erskine (1685–1752) was a minister in Dunfermline and a leading pastor in the Secession of 1733. Erskine was diligent in his parish responsibilities; he and a colleague annually examined the public and visited families for a parish of over 5,000.

6. Andrew Donaldson was minister of Dalgety, Scotland, from 1644 to 1662.

7. John Willison (1680–1750) was a Church of Scotland minister in Brechin and Dundee South. He is remembered chiefly for his devotional writings, but he participated in two major revivals and was a staunch opponent of Moderatism (see note 4).

8. Thomas Boston (1676–1732) was a Church of Scotland minister and theologian. He is closely associated with the parish of Ettrick, where for 25 years he preached covenant theology, the free offer of the gospel, and faith in Christ as the assurance of salvation. He is chiefly remembered for his role in the Marrow Controversy (1717–1723) and for *Human Nature in Its Fourfold State* (1720, 1729), the most widely published Scottish book of the eighteenth century.

We need no new machinery in the Christian church. It is all provided ready to our hand in the Presbyterian system. What we need is motive-power to set it going and keep it going. We need the baptism of the Spirit to fill us elders with love and zeal, that we may labor in our office and that the work of our hands may be established.

The eldership, under some form or other, is absolutely necessary for a healthy and useful church. The Wesleyans have adopted it largely in the form of class leaders. Many Baptist and Congregational churches expect their deacons to do elders' work.[9] And many intelligent Episcopalians desire to have lay agency formally sanctioned in their churches. That union of order and liberty so distinguishing our elastic Presbyterian system—which is not, like our limited monarchy, the result of the experience of ages, but was, as we believe, laid down in the New Testament eighteen hundred years ago—will bear the test of practical trial in every land.[10]

So necessary is the eldership for the superintendence of a congregation that practical wisdom would demand it even if Scripture did not provide it. In ordinary congregations it is physically impossible for the ministers to do all that is needful, or they must cease to give themselves to prayer and the ministry of the Word. It is expected that our ministers prepare two sermons or lectures every week, and that these be the result of much study and thought. We do not enter on the

9. Happily, in our day some Baptist churches are recovering the office of elder, biblically understood.

10. Dickson's point is that like the political form of government known as limited monarchy, Presbyterianism allows for maximum liberty while at the same time preserving order in the church. Of course, the reasons for following this form of church government are not merely practical, but also biblical.

question whether this is reasonable in all circumstances or for spiritual edification; we merely take things as they are. And besides the weekly preparation of two discourses, the minister is expected to visit his whole flock in succession, especially attending to the sick. Then he has other duties as a public servant of Christ. It is therefore utterly impossible for him, singly and alone, to care for several hundred souls as they ought to be cared for.

Our people know well the necessity and usefulness of the office of the eldership. All over Scotland there is a happy prejudice in favor of an elder's visit. No elder could ever say that they did not welcome his visits. The houses and hearts of the people are ever open to those whom they have called to the office. "I am very glad to see you" will be the salutation in every case. Next to faith in God, let us have trust in our people—our discouragements in duty seldom come from *them*.

Because our object is not a controversial but a practical one, we do not enter on the Scripture argument for the office of the eldership. Should anyone wish to study the subject, we may refer him to the work of Dr. Lorimer,[11] embodying the excellent tract on this subject by James Guthrie of Stirling, the honored martyr of the second Reformation;[12] also to the learned

11. John Gordon Lorimer (1804–1868) was a Free Church minister and writer from Haddington and served as the pastor of St. David's Church in Glasgow from 1832 to his death. He wrote *The Eldership of the Church of Scotland* (1832) and *The Deaconship* (1842).

12. James Guthrie (1612–1661) was the Scottish minister and staunch Presbyterian who wrote *A Treatise of Ruling Elders and Deacons* (1652). Guthrie signed the National Covenant of 1638 and remained politically active throughout the reigns of Charles I and Charles II. As Dickson suggests, he was executed in 1660 when the monarchy was restored and Charles II led the Scottish church away from Presbyterianism and back toward an Episcopal form of church government.

and most useful treatise on the office of ruling elder by Dr. Miller of Princeton, New Jersey;[13] to the work of the late Dr. M'Kerrow, which gained the prize offered for the best treatise on the subject by a devoted and liberal elder of the United Presbyterian Church in Edinburgh;[14] and last, not least, to the eminently practical volume from the pen of Dr. King.[15]

13. Samuel Miller (1769–1850) was a Presbyterian minister in New York City and later professor of church history at Princeton Theological Seminary. The treatise that Dickson mentions was entitled *Essay on the Warrant, Nature and Duties of the Office of the Ruling Elder in the Presbyterian Church* (1831).

14. John M'Kerrow (1789–1867) was a Scottish minister; the manuscript referred to here was published as *The Office of Ruling Elder in the Christian Church: Its Divine Authority and Responsibilities* (1846).

15. David King (1806–1883) wrote *Ruling Eldership of the Christian Church.*

Study Questions

1. What terms does the Bible use for the office of elder (see Acts 20:17, 28)? What does each term teach us about the elder's calling? These terms are used synonymously: what does this usage teach us about church governance?

2. Elders must give account for the souls under their care (Heb. 13:17). What does this mean? What are elders accountable before God to do?

3. The Bible also instructs elders to "take heed unto themselves" (Acts 20:28). Keeping this command requires careful self-examination. How closely are you walking with God at home? At work? In the church? In your own relationship with Christ? Give specific examples of your progress in godliness.

4. Why is biblical eldership necessary for a healthy and useful church?

2

THE ELDER'S QUALIFICATIONS

Before referring to duties, it may be profitable to dwell a little on the qualifications required for the elder's office, as we gather these from the epistles to Timothy and Titus, from Peter's first epistle, and from other passages of Scripture.

1. The office and work being spiritual, it is necessary that elders should be spiritual men. It is not necessary that they be men of great gifts or worldly position, of wealth or high education, but it is indispensably necessary that they be men of God, at peace with him, new creatures in Christ Jesus; engaged in the embassy of reconciliation, they must be themselves reconciled. We must love the Master, and the work for the Master's sake. If we do love it, it will be a happy service because it is a willing service. And as our souls prosper, our work will prosper; the joy of the Lord will be our strength.

Let us "take heed unto ourselves" (Acts 20:28) as to our real state of heart and our motives. Are we living branches of the true Vine (John 15:1–11), and are we growing? Though the work of the eldership is in itself very honorable and very interesting, yet it will be dull, formal, and worthless unless there is a real and growing love to Jesus in our hearts. That is the only oil that will make the lamp burn and keep it burning. We must be men of prayer if we are to honor the Lord in our office. And we must have the word of Christ dwelling in us richly (cf. Col. 3:16), studying especially the details of his own ministry on earth and such chapters as the twelfth of Romans and the thirteenth of First Corinthians.[1]

2. We should have a good knowledge of the Word of God, and be able to give a reason for the hope that is in us. Not that we must be theologians, able to grapple learnedly with all heresies or controversies; but we should be well read in our Bibles, and able to do what Aquila and Priscilla did to Apollos.[2] Elders should be men to a certain extent "established, strengthened, settled" (1 Peter 5:10), not "novices" (1 Tim. 3:6), whom the elevation to office in the church is likely to make heady, forward, crotchety, conceited. For very young men and very young Christians, other useful though humbler spheres are more suitable. It is a very great help to an elder to have been for some years previously a Sabbath-school teacher, and thus accustomed to study the truth and to apply it. Such work will also test his intelligence and interest in divine things. If an elder is to discharge the duty laid upon him in Scripture—"to reprove, rebuke and exhort" (2 Tim.

---

1. Romans 12 discusses the practical implications of offering our bodies "as a living sacrifice, holy and acceptable to God" (Rom. 12:1 ESV). 1 Corinthians 13 is the Bible's famous love chapter. Dickson specifies these passages because the person and work of the elder should be characterized by sacrificial love.

2. Aquila and Priscilla instructed Apollos so that he would gain a more adequate understanding of Christian doctrine (Acts 18:26).

4:2), to "be able by sound doctrine to exhort and convince gainsayers" (Titus 1:9)—the Word of God must be the man of his counsel, his daily companion.

Let me not be thought to discourage elders from the study of theology as a systematic science. Anyone who has studied the Westminster Confession of Faith, as all elders should do, is no mean theologian. And it is a great strength to the church of Christ that many of her laymen (as they may be called, for want of a better word) should be well up in doctrinal controversy. Elders who have time and ability for this should give themselves to it. No heresy ever becomes extinct, as some volcanoes are said to do, for they all come out of the old human heart, which is as full of evil as ever. But the old heresies assume new forms well worthy of study and detection; and the world listens to an exposure of them more readily from laymen than from ministers, even though not half so able or conclusive.

3. Elders should be men of common sense, knowing when to speak and when to hold their tongues. Even grace does not give common sense, a little of which would settle many controversies and heresies in the church of Christ. Men of points and pugnacity are very annoying in a session or congregation, and they may rise to be the terror of presbyteries and other church courts. They may love the truth at heart—and we believe they often do—but they love fighting too. For such men the grave and quiet duties of the eldership have little or no charm. A carping, censorious spirit is to be watched and prayed against in all of us: it is often the precursor or companion of backsliding in doctrine or life. An uneasy conscience likes to find faults in others. Having many different characters and tempers to deal with, we need as elders to be men of a meek and quiet spirit, not going from one extreme to another—men

of practical wisdom and sanctified common sense, and thus able to judge matters calmly and not as partisans.

4. We must be consistent in our life and conversation; we must be clean that bear the vessels of the Lord (Isa. 52:11); men of "good report" (1 Tim. 3:7), both with those who are without and those who are within the church; model members of it; "examples to the flock" (1 Peter 5:3) in faith, hope, and charity, ruling our own children and our own houses well. In these days wolves find it profitable to put on sheep's clothing, for a certain amount of religious profession is a help and not a hindrance to a man's worldly prosperity. The church and the world are thus in danger of fraternizing, and it is always the church that loses.

Let us elders avoid all appearance of evil. Let us be known in business as men whose word is as good as our bond—not mean or shabby in our dealings, not considered hard or money-loving men (which brings greater reproach on the Christian name than even the cases of flagrant hypocrisy that sometimes occur), but willing to let go the doubtful penny,[3] as becomes God's royal priesthood (1 Peter 2:9), whose treasure is in heaven.

Let us by our daily life declare plainly that we "seek a country" (Heb. 11:16) by our being sober, just, holy, temperate. Let us be liberal [i.e., generous] to Christ's cause according to our ability; attached to our own church and our own congregation, and at the same time lovers of all good men and good causes, for the man who loves his own family best has usually most room in his heart for those outside of it; given to hospitality and seeking to make our house a home for God's people.

3. By "the doubtful penny," Dickson means money obtained through some morally questionable means.

The usefulness of an elder will depend in the long run more on his character than on his gifts and knowledge. Quiet Christian consistency will give weight to his words of advice and be a daily lesson to all around. His walk and conversation, his style of living, his companions and friends, his geniality, his amusements will all have an important influence, not only on his own family, but on the people of his district and congregation.[4] Young people especially notice, and get good or evil from, much that they do not speak about to others. They should learn from us what a Christian is like, not by the frequent use of certain pious expressions, but by the clear, transparent outflow of a life "hid with Christ in God" (Col. 3:3). Brethren, "what manner of persons ought we elders to be in all holy conversation and godliness?" (2 Peter 3:11).

5. Last, not least, we should be men of deep sympathy—having not only human kindness in our hearts, but that sanctified and consecrated. Having experience of the ups and downs of human life, we should have sympathy with human hearts, ready ever to "weep with them that weep and rejoice with them that rejoice" (Rom. 12:15). The world is not governed by logic, and to do much good in it, especially as Christian men and elders, the words of truth we speak must come warm from our hearts, or they fall cold and pointless. It was once said to me of another, "He's a good man, but somehow he never reminds me of Jesus." Much of our usefulness will lie not only in knowing the wants, natural and spiritual, of

---

4. When he speaks of an elder's "district," Dickson is referring to geographic divisions in the city of Edinburgh: each elder cared for the people in his own district. Most of his comments about the elder's work in his district would apply equally well to other methods of subdividing a congregation (cell groups, mini-churches, shepherding folds, care groups, etc.).

our people, but in our having that heart-sympathy with them that will make us open our hearts to them, and will lead them to open their minds and hearts to us in return. We can best learn this by living in fellowship with him who was displeased with his disciples when they rebuked the mothers for bringing their little children to him (Matt. 19:13–14), and when they wished the hungry multitude to be sent away unfed (Matt. 14:13–16).

Study Questions

1. What qualifications does your church consider in the election of elders? How closely does your list of formal and informal requirements for the office of elder match the biblical pattern?

2. Elders must be spiritual men. What evidence do you see that you are a man of God? List some ways in which you are growing in the gospel.

3. What practical steps are you taking to improve your knowledge of God's Word? Your grasp of biblical and systematic theology?

4. Elders must be careful not to develop an appetite for conflict and controversy. What individuals or issues are most likely to frustrate you, or even arouse your anger? What are some godly ways to handle these people and problems?

5. Dickson claims that an elder's usefulness depends more on his character than on his gifts. Do you agree or disagree with this claim? How would you defend your answer?

6. "He's a good man, but somehow he never reminds me of Jesus." Use this statement as a basis for self-examination. What kind of example are you setting for the people in your church and community? In what ways are you *least* likely to remind people of Jesus? List some practical steps you can take to grow in these areas.

3

DUTIES OF ELDERS

The following extract from an act of the General Assembly of the Free Church of Scotland, passed in 1846, gives an excellent summary of the duties of elders:

1. That they sit in session along with the minister, and assist in the administration of discipline and in the spiritual government of the church.
2. That they take a careful oversight of the people's morals and religious principles, of the attendance upon public ordinances, and of the state of personal and family religion.
3. That they visit the sick from time to time in their several districts.
4. That they superintend the religious instruction of the young, and assist the minister in ascertaining the qualifications of applicants for admission to sealing ordinances.
5. That they superintend and promote the formation of meetings within their districts for prayer, reading of the Scriptures, and Christian fellowship among the members of the church.

The elder labors under two great disadvantages. In the first place, while he has a general idea of the work to which he has been set apart, there is no prescribed or understood plan laid down for him in the doing of it. Each elder has thus been left to do what seemed right in his own eyes. Any fixed plan it would be impossible to lay down, as every elder, every district, and every congregation differs so much from every other. We can therefore easily understand how elders who are timid or inexperienced feel a difficulty, and do much less than they might do.

Another disadvantage is that the time when he should visit his district is not naturally suggested. A minister once said to us regretfully, in reference to his weekday duties, "No bell rings me to my work." The remark applies still more to an elder. No bell, not even the Sabbath-bell, rings him to his work; he can do it at any time. There is no day or hour that naturally reminds him of his duty, a disadvantage under which a deacon or Sabbath-school teacher does not labor. No wonder that with some of us the *any time* becomes the *no time*, and especially if we have never so engaged in the work as to have known the blessedness and enjoyment of it.

We do not suggest that our churches should lay down rules, as to either details of the work that elders should do or the time when they should do it. There are many reasonable objections to this. We would rather seek, by bringing under the notice of elders the various plans by which elders of different churches and congregations seek to discharge their duty, to furnish hints as to how we may in our several spheres use the office to which we have been ordained for the good of the souls committed to our care.

The time required for the efficient discharge of the elder's duties is not great, especially where the office of the deacon is established. On the average, and generally speaking, two hours a week might be enough, perhaps even less. Most Christian men should be able and willing thus to give one-fiftieth part of their weekday waking hours to this work, and we are sure that neither their family nor their business would be loser.

Our object is to gather together and place before the minds of our brethren in the eldership useful methods that have been or might be taken for doing good in their respective districts. Some of them are new, but most of them have been successfully used by elders in various spheres and various churches. It is one of the evils of our want of cooperation as churches that good plans are employed by one church or by one elder that, if only made known, would at once commend themselves to others.

Of course, no one will imagine that all the various plans are applicable to all districts. Dr. Elder of Rothesay remarks (in an admirable address to elders published some years ago, from which I have taken several useful hints): "The eldership exhibits the greatest possible variety in respect of outward circumstances, of natural and spiritual gifts and of means and capabilities of usefulness. It is one of the many excellencies of our Presbyterian system that it draws its office-bearers out of all classes of its membership, from the noble to the peasant, from the merchant-prince to the humble artisan, from the philosopher down to the lowly cottager who has no learning but that which is of God."[1]

1. Robert Elder (1808–1892) served as minister of the Free Church of Scotland at Kilbrandon, Killin, and Rothesay. He was moderator of the Free Church in 1871.

Then our districts differ very widely, as do the congregations of which they form parts, whether in town or country, urban or suburban, composed of the upper, middle, or working classes. These differences make it essential that prayerful wisdom should guide each elder, or at least each church session, to decide as to what plans of usefulness are suitable in each case. It is "as we have opportunity" that we are "to do good unto all men" (Gal. 6:10). Let us set our ingenuity to work, that we may be able in the best sense to be all things to all men, that we may save some. In any way, and every way consistent with Scripture and good sense, let us aim at this great end.

Study Questions

1. Review Dickson's list of the duties of elders. Is there anything you would add? Which duties seem to be the focus for elders in your church? In your own ministry, which duty or duties need more careful attention?

2. Dickson suggests that the average elder needs only two hours a week to discharge his duties. Is this a reasonable estimate? What does your church expect of its elders?

3. Evaluate your use of time. Are you faithfully fulfilling the demands of your calling? How can you organize your schedule to become a more effective servant of the church? This is a good topic to discuss with a friend or colleague (and also your wife, if you are married).

4

The Elder in His District

The size of districts is an important matter. If a district is too small, the elder is apt to underestimate the importance of his work; if too large, he is apt to think that it cannot possibly be overtaken, and thus to do less than he might do. In the allotment of districts, care should be taken by the session that the residence and qualifications of each elder are suitable to the district assigned to him; the right man should be put in the right place.

In large congregations, besides the local district elders, some of the brethren who have suitable qualifications might be appointed to *duties* instead of *districts*, such as the superintendence of the congregational Sabbath school or of the district mission, the oversight of servants (a very migratory class), the care of the widows or orphans, of students or young men coming from the country.

Too much care cannot be taken that additions to the congregation at each communion and at other times be regularly intimated to the district elders, and also that elders should intimate the removal of members from one district of the congregation to another. We believe that a considerable loss in funds is sustained by the neglect of this and, what is much more serious, that many persons and families have been allowed thus to drift away from church connection altogether. It is best, at least in large congregations, that all intimations of removal from one district to another be made to the session clerk, and by him transmitted to the elder of the new district, as well as to the minister.

In addition to the communicants' roll, kept alphabetically, it is well that the session clerk keep a list of members arranged in districts. From this the elders can at any time correct their district lists. In some congregations a list of the members and adherents in each district is printed annually for the use of the office-bearers and collectors.

An elder's district roll should contain the names of all the members of the families, not only of those who are communicants, but of all the children. It should show those who have communicated [i.e. received communion] at each sacramental season, and the dates of his visits to each family.[1] Various elders' visiting books have been prepared, but probably each elder will do best by making a plan for himself. He should avoid burdening himself with needless statistics. He will find it useful to know where his people sit in church. If possible, every elder should personally know every member of the congregation, which in our smaller congregations it will not be difficult for him to do.

---

1. For centuries it was customary for Presbyterian churches in Scotland and elsewhere to keep careful records of members participating in the Lord's Supper, which in many churches was celebrated only once or twice a year.

If the great ends of our office are, by God's blessing, to be attained, it is plain, in the first place, that the elder must know the people in his district. He must be acquainted with them all, old and young, their history, their occupations, their habits, their ways of thinking. They and their children should be his personal friends, so that they naturally turn to him as to one on whom they can depend as a kind and sympathizing friend and a faithful counselor. He must know them as they are at home, at their own fireside. As Dr. Chalmers said, "The way into a man's heart is in at the door of his house."[2] And he must keep up this knowledge by visiting them from time to time.

On entering on his work at first, and as new people come into his district, an elder must endeavor to get into conversation with them individually as to the state of their souls. Is the great question yet settled? Have they said *yes* or *no* to the message of peace on earth and goodwill to men? Elders often feel it difficult to get into this kind of conversation. It should be done, of course, privately, prudently, tenderly; yet it *should* be done—not in the spirit of "Stand by, for I am holier than thou," but of one who is greatly concerned about their eternal interests. Let us not be content with mere generalities, for

2. The famous preacher, theologian, and social reformer Thomas Chalmers (1780–1847) is generally regarded as Scotland's greatest churchman of the nineteenth century. He is perhaps best known for his revitalization of parish life in Glasgow, where he served as minister of the Tron and other churches before proceeding to prestigious academic posts at Saint Andrews and New College, Edinburgh. Like David Dickson, Chalmers believed that the degradations of industrialized society could best be ameliorated through the gospel ministry, and he helped organize the city into small parishes ("proportions," as he called them) so that the church and not the government could attend to the spiritual and material needs of the urban poor.

our visits are not those of ceremony or merely of courtesy; we have a great business in hand—*the* great business.

Such conversation, if in the spirit of our Master, will usually be well received, and is often much blessed. Those who are God's children will feel thankful that they have found one to whom they can open their hearts; and those who have but a name to live—their name on the communion roll only—may be led to fall in with God's way of saving sinners.[3] Many even in this Christian land live twenty, thirty, or forty years before they meet with anyone who speaks to them directly and personally about their soul's salvation. How backward and shy (alas!) are we all to do this! To speak thus with good results, our words must be accompanied with prayer and a consistent life. May the Lord baptize us elders with such a spirit of love and power that we shall be able to speak to every one of our people about their soul's salvation, so that none shall ever be able to say, "He visited me often, but he never spoke *plainly* to me about the state of my soul." Alas! is there any of us who can say in this matter, "I am pure from the blood of all men" (Acts 20:26)?

Don't let us take too much for granted. So strange to the natural heart is the idea of salvation by another's righteousness that we believe no one really understands it, even intellectually, till taught by the Spirit. Ignorant of God's righteousness, of the King's highway, we would fain go to heaven by a road that was shut up more than five thousand years ago. An old Moderate minister in preaching used to define faith as "a belief in the being and attributes of God; and if any man," said he, "says it is more, don't believe him, for that

3. Dickson's concern here is with people who are members of the visible church but do not have a personal saving faith in Jesus Christ.

would just mean the getting of another to do what every man should do for himself."[4] This was natural religion, the religion of the natural heart. An old woman who was born again at the age of eighty-two once told me that though she had sat for sixty years under most faithful ministers, her mind never really understood God's way of saving sinners till the Spirit taught her "heaven's easy, artless, unencumbered plan"— "Believe and live."

When Dr. M'Donald of Ferrintosh, the apostle of the North, was minister of the Gaelic church in Edinburgh, he used to frequent a bookseller's shop in the South Bridge. To one of the lads in the shop he sometimes used to drop a kind and gracious word about the great salvation. That lad lived to be an old man, and has often told me that he looked on Dr. M'Donald as his spiritual father. But the lesson was blessed in more ways than one. The disciple also learned to give a word in season to others. A youth was one day showing him a picture of a lonely cottage on a moor, and said, "How can anyone live there?" The reply was the beginning of a new life. It was this: "John, we can live *anywhere* if we have Christ in us and Christ with us." Many other instances could be given of a blessing attending personal dealing with individuals about "the great concern."[5]

4. For a concise definition of Moderatism, see note 4. Here Dickson is arguing against the Moderate position that salvation depends on obeying God for ourselves rather than trusting in the righteousness of Jesus Christ, imputed to us by faith.

5. John Macdonald (1779–1849) was a leading preacher in the Scottish Highlands during the first half of the nineteenth century. His evangelistic campaigns earned him the title that Dickson uses here: "Apostle of the North."

Study Questions

1. Is your congregation effectively organized for spiritual care? If not, what can be done to improve your plan for shepherding God's flock?

2. "The right man should be put in the right place." How does your session divide its duties? Is there a good match between the gifts of your elders and the places they are called to serve?

3. Effective elders know how to engage people in spiritual conversation. List several good questions that an elder can ask to evaluate the spiritual condition of the people under his care.

4. "May the Lord baptize us elders with such a spirit of love and power that we shall be able to speak to every one of our people about their soul's salvation." Evaluate several of the conversations you have had with church members and others during recent weeks and months. In what ways have you shown a concern for their eternal destiny?

5

ORDINARY VISITATION BY THE ELDER

The frequency of an elder's ordinary visitation must depend on the nature of the district, the time at his disposal, and the mode of his visitation. Some visit throughout their districts every three months, but perhaps in most cases a half-yearly visit may be found sufficient. Be it more or less frequent, however, every elder should have a plan, and keep to it. The day and hour selected should, of course, be convenient for the people, when domestic arrangements will not be disturbed and the household are likely to be all at home. Some elders send previous intimation of their intention to visit, but the visit will be more easy and natural to both elder and people when paid without previous notice.

Of late years it has been the practice in many congregations to dispense with the old custom of giving out tokens, substituting instead the plan of distributing communicants' cards before each communion. One great advantage of this is that it ensures, when faithfully carried out, the periodical visitation of all the members. In some congregations the cards are exchanged for tokens at a diet of worship immediately before the communion; in other cases they are not, but are used in place of tokens.[1]

The experience of those who have tried it is on the whole in favor of the plan of communicants' cards. It would be liable to no objection if elders began so early in their distribution as to be able with them to make a real visitation of their districts every six months, spending perhaps half an hour with each household. There is, of course, the manifest danger of procrastination, or the elder being prevented by illness or other urgent engagements. If the cards have to be distributed at the eleventh hour by a hasty call at the door, like that of the postman or tax collector, all that can be said is that it is better than no visit at all. If done, however, punctually and conscientiously, this system works well, securing accuracy in names and addresses of members, and ascertaining those who actually communicate [i.e. received communion]. And certainly no time is more suitable for visiting our people than just before a communion.

An elder should visit all the people, rich as well as poor. He is apt to visit most frequently where he is most warmly welcomed, but these are not always the families to whom he may be most useful. Neither should he visit chiefly the poorer members. The richer people are apt to be neglected by the elder. There are many people well off, as this world goes, who are very lonely, much needing sympathy and Christian kind-

1. During the nineteenth century, many Scottish churches celebrated communion only once or twice a year. In order to receive the sacrament, members had to present cards or tokens indicating that they had their elder's approval to commune. This was designed to promote good spiritual care and maintain church discipline. In order for the system to work effectively, however, elders had to be diligent in meeting with their parishioners and examining them prior to communion.

ness, to whom a cheerful visitor can carry sunshine and blessing. And a lonely life has its own evils and temptations, requiring counsel and direction. A Christian lady once remarked to me long ago, "If I were a poor body I would often get a visit from my elder, but if all were known I need it as much as anyone." Visits to the better class are most useful to the elder himself. Visiting only the poorer is easier, but not more useful.

While endeavoring to keep to a plan of full and regular visitation, an elder must not think that a short visit occasionally is of no use. This would be a great mistake. If we are intimate with our people, we can often do much good by a kindly look-in, even though we scarcely sit down in the house.

Let us never seem when visiting as if we grudged every moment, as if we were fidgeting to get away—a habit both rude and injurious. When we come into a house, we should seek to bring some of heaven's own sunshine into it. The children must not run away and hide themselves, but be the first to welcome us; for, like their fathers and mothers, they should be all our personal friends.

Our conversation when visiting should be suitable to our office and our object. It cannot be too genial and lively,[2] provided it is as becomes the gospel of Christ. "The talk of the lips tendeth only to penury" (Prov. 14:23); "Let your speech be always with grace, seasoned with salt" (Col. 4:6); "Be kindly-affectioned one to another, with brotherly love" (Rom. 12:10)—these are some of the texts that may guide us as to our conversation. It should be profitable, yet pleasant, lively, and interesting—grace seasoned with salt. We should avoid

2. In other words, elders should be as genial and as lively as possible!

stiffness and formality, still more moroseness or affected solemnity, for we must get at our people's hearts if we are to do them any good.

Cheerfulness becomes the saints, and we would be more cheerful if we walked all the day in the light of his countenance. We would thus present, especially to young people, truth with a winsome face. A good woman who made her living by keeping lodgers told me that the constant cheerfulness of a Christian young man who was a lodger in her house was the first means of awakening her. She saw that there was a fountain of joy in his heart to which she was a stranger. Did you ever observe the power of a pleasant, genial, or even humorous remark in opening the fissures of the human heart so as to let you drop in some seed of divine truth? Avoiding foolish talking and jesting, which are never convenient, a vein of humor is a great gift for Christ if ballasted with discretion and humility. Mr. Spurgeon is an example of this,[3] as others have been. A healthy mind and soul are seldom without a little of it.

In her early years, a friend of mine used to meet with Wilberforce.[4] Few men were ever more useful to individuals; and it was by his "parlor preaching," which consisted,

3. Charles Spurgeon (1834–1892) was the famous Baptist minister who preached to large crowds at the New Park Street Baptist Church in London from 1854 to 1861 and the Metropolitan Tabernacle from 1861 to 1891. He often visited Scotland and frequently spent his summers in the North Country. Although he often battled dark depression, Spurgeon was cheerful and high-spirited in public.

4. William Wilberforce (1759–1833) was an evangelical Christian in the Church of England who joined with the English Quakers to form the Society for the Abolition of the Slave Trade. The Society annually proposed abolitionist bills to Parliament, finally meeting with success in 1807, when slavery was abolished.

as my friend told me, in his geniality and humor being sanctified to the highest service. In the midst of his public work he never avoided mixing freely with the society around him, knowing that there he had a large sphere of usefulness. The tendency in some men to keep themselves aloof from pleasant social intercourse with the circle of kindred and friendship with which God has surrounded them, on the plea that they have no time for it, has no sanction from our Lord's precept and example. They should have time for it, for it is by contact that the leaven spreads till the whole is leavened (Matt. 13:33).

The matter of our social intercourse is fully as important as the manner of it. While we may talk about congregational matters, let us beware of congregational gossip. "Is it really true that Mr. A. is going to be married to Miss B.?" is one of the kinds of questions that should be neither asked nor answered. We should avoid, if possible, all talk about persons, especially neighbors, unless we can speak well of them and to edification. Let the elder forestall all this kind of thing by reference to the last Sabbath sermons, the work of the congregation, or some news in the last Record or other religious periodicals.[5] Even in the events of the day and their lessons we may, in these times of daily newspapers and telegraphs, find ample scope for most profitable conversation. Let us throw out hints that may be useful, such as the importance of reading regularly through the sixty-six books of the Bible, and not trusting to little "text-books."[6]

5. The *Record of the Home and Foreign Mission Work* was published by the United Free Church of Scotland.

6. Here Dickson refers to booklets and pamphlets containing verses or chapters from Scripture; he wanted people to read the whole Bible, not just parts of it.

We have already referred to the duty of every faithful elder dealing personally with each member of a family. This must be done privately, yet even when the children are present there will be many opportunities for earnest religious conversation. Young anxious inquirers may be there, secretly wishing you to speak of what is near their hearts, though, with the reticence of many people on these subjects, they may never have opened their minds even to their father or mother. I remember once getting a quiet reproof on this point from a Christian mother. After some too desultory conversation I proposed to read a passage of Scripture. "Oh," said she, "I was wondering if you were going away without that, for I have lately felt very anxious about the souls of my children." How often do our coldness and shyness as to the one thing needful prevent our usefulness!

Our visits should be "sanctified by the word of God and prayer" (1 Tim. 4:5), though it should not be considered indispensable that at every visit we should conduct a formal exercise. We may read a passage, and if we can add a few remarks on it, so much the better, but they should be homely, practical, interesting, and brief. It may be enough at times merely to quote a text. In prayer we should avoid a long preface or peroration, or other formalities. The circumstances of the family and of each member of it, present or absent, should be specially remembered.

In visiting we may find some strangers present, people staying with the family or neighbors who have looked in. Let us try to have a word for them. They may have been thrown in our way for that very purpose. A friend once told me of a neighbor who came into a house during his visit, and was arrested by a text that was read. Such simple means does the Lord often use to find his lost pieces of silver (Luke 15:8–10).

For several years I have adopted a plan in which I have had much comfort and satisfaction. I know that with some of my brethren it would not be practicable, though others might adopt it. The plan I refer to is spending an hour every Sabbath evening with one family in my district. Having ascertained at church that it will be convenient for the family to receive me that evening, after my own family exercise I go to the house at eight o'clock. If there are children there, the first thing I do is to catechize them a little, which they and the parents seem to enter into very heartily. Besides the instruction conveyed to the children, I find thus an opportunity of giving hints to the parents as to the matter and manner of family religious instruction. This being over, I have a short exercise for all, such as family worship, praise, reading a short passage of Scripture, with a few remarks for old and young, and prayer, especially remembering any of the family who have left home. The children then leaving us, there is a little time for conversation with the father and mother.

Never have I come home from one of these Sabbath-evening visits without feeling thankful that I had been led to begin this plan, and that it was lawful thus to do good on the Sabbath day. It is the best time for the elder, for the rest and privileges of the Sabbath have put his heart in tune for such employment. And it is best for the family; they are all at home, disengaged, expecting us, and not likely to be disturbed. How good and pleasant it is thus to go in upon a family at their quiet fireside on a Sabbath evening, the family Bible on the table ready for us, the whole reminding us of that family religion that once made Scotland great and good, and that, if continued and renewed, would make her still a joy and blessing to the whole earth! The family—how much of a nation's happiness and prosperity depends on that institution as a nursery, a school, a society, a sanctuary, a little church, and an emblem of the great family—"the whole family" (Eph. 3:15), part of which is in heaven, and part still on earth!

There are other matters we should keep in view in our visitation to families, which will be referred to afterward.

Study Questions

1. What plan does your church have for ordinary pastoral visitation? How effectively is this plan being carried out?

2. "An elder should visit *all* the people." Which members of your congregation are most likely to be overlooked or neglected? Is there anyone you need to make special plans to visit?

3. What practical advice does David Dickson give for making an effective elder visit? Is there anything you would add to his suggestions? What is the best place or time for you to visit the people in your congregation?

4. Evaluate the personal time you have spent with church members in recent months. Have your conversations focused on spiritual things? Did you make good use of Scripture? Are you developing friendly relationships with children?

6

VISITATION OF THE SICK

In every district there are usually some invalids from age, infirmity, or protracted disease, and a sickbed life is not necessarily good for the soul. Deprived of the privileges of God's house, and often very lonely, they require more frequent visits than ordinary families, and have a special claim on an elder's time and sympathy. Often weak and sensitive, they are very susceptible of kindness, and grateful for it. Some may require systematic instruction in the truth; and even where this is not necessary, the elder will find that it adds greater usefulness and interest to his successive visits to speak a little on some one important truth; he will not find this without fruit. I believe sickbed conversions are numerous, and even deathbed conversions (so far as man can judge) sometimes occur. Apart from all such cases, every elder knows that on the bed of sickness the Lord ripens his people for glory, and to the elder himself it is often a scene of instruction and revival. Richard Cecil said that some of the best lessons he had ever learned were had at the sickbeds of believers; and many elders can say the same.[1]

---

1. The published work of the English revivalist Richard Cecil (1748–1810) includes *Friendly Advice from a Minister to the Servant of His Parish* (1793) and *Character and Commendation of the Faithful Minister* (1808; a sermon on the death of John Newton).

Besides giving them the varied comfort and direction so abundant in the Word of life, he may lend them suitable books. He should also enlist the help of some Christian neighbor, who, if kind, cheerful, and experienced in divine things, may be more useful in some respects than he could be. Such, at least, has been my own experience. Nervous weakness tells upon the soul, and visits to invalids by children, for example, who can sing to the weary sufferers some of the sweet songs of Zion (Ps. 137:3), may do more good, even to the body, than medicines from the druggist's shop.

An elder told me lately that he usually spent some hours of every New Year's Day in visiting sick friends, taking with him little gifts, which, with kind words, would cheer and revive many to whom a holiday brings no gladness of heart. This is a good hint as to how to make a holiday a happy day even to ourselves, for "it is more blessed to give than to receive" (Acts 20:35).

In visiting sick people or invalids, we should avoid noise or abruptness. A low, quiet voice is usually soothing and pleasant to them, especially if they are weak and nervous. Don't let us strain them with anything requiring long or continuous attention, and let our change from one subject to another be natural and easy. Such visits should not be of long duration, and it is best for us to leave immediately after engaging in prayer, giving them perhaps *one* text to keep near their heart.

It is a good plan occasionally to have a short service in the sickroom of an invalid, to which a few neighbors may be invited. Invalids seem to enjoy this very much; it reminds them of the joy they once had in going up to the house of God; and it is social worship when two or three are thus gathered together in the name of Jesus.

Cases of urgent and serious illness require, of course, an elder's special attention. "Is any sick among you? Let him call for the elders of the church" (James 5:14). It is to be regretted that the sufferer or his family does not always comply with this injunction, under the mistaken impression that the elder *ought* to hear of them, though such a thing is not expected of the doctor of a family. But when the elder does hear of such illness, he should visit *at once*. A day's, or even an hour's, unnecessary delay may cause him a long regret.[2] He should see that the minister is also made aware of the case as soon as possible.

To visit the fatherless and widows in their affliction is our privilege and duty, and to carry with us such messages from the Word of God as are fitted to bind up the broken heart. In cases of sudden and severe affliction, we may be able to do little more than weep with them that weep (Rom. 12:15), giving the afflicted some word from the merciful and faithful High Priest, and perhaps taking hold of the sufferer's hand—an act of sympathy that often has a wonderful power to calm and soothe in times of deep distress.

We know very little about those ministering spirits who are sent forth to minister for those who are heirs of salvation (i.e., angels; Heb. 1:14). But may we not be often side by side with them? For this is our privilege as well as theirs. And it is our part, being ourselves also in the body (1 Cor. 12:12; Rom. 12:5), to do what they are not privileged to do—to sit beside a dying believer, to smooth his pillow, to moisten his lips, to remind him of the rod and staff that are ready for his help in the dark valley (Ps. 23:4), and to direct his dying eye

2. Dickson was writing at a time when even ordinary illnesses not infrequently ended in death.

to Jesus. All this is a precious service we cannot render in heaven, but only on earth.

Have we realized the honor and privilege given us by our Lord of ministering to an heir of salvation? Would we like to have shown kindness to Jesus himself, who for our sakes became poor? Would we like our roof to have sheltered him, our fire to have warmed him, our food to have fed him? This service of love is still within our reach, for "inasmuch as ye have done it unto one of the least of *these my brethren*, ye did it unto me" (Matt. 25:40).

> Oh that the Lord would count me meet
> To wash his dear disciples' feet;
> After my lowly Lord to go,
> And wait upon his saints below;
> Enjoy the grace to angels given,
> And serve the royal heirs of heaven!

The elder will seek, along with the minister, that a time of affliction may be a time of blessing to a family. It is not necessarily so, nor always so, for trial is not in itself sanctifying. But at such a time the affections are stirred and the mind opened to hear what would not have been listened to at another time. It is often a crisis in a family's history. Let us seek wisdom to win souls at such a time; kindness and sympathy from us *then* will never be forgotten. It is after the excitement is over that a bereavement is most felt. The empty chair, the quiet home, remind the widow and the orphan of their loneliness. Let the bereaved ones feel that in this cold and selfish world they have in their elder at least one human friend left. We may look in upon them in the evening occasionally and conduct the family worship, trying in some measure to fulfill the promise, "When my father and mother forsake me, then the LORD will take me up" (Ps. 27:10).

And let us share in family joys as well as sorrows. I like to be invited to a marriage in my district, for it shows a kinship feeling toward me. If we are intimate with our people, we will often be asked for advice in such matters, and we may help in steering them clear of rocks and quicksands. Let us remember the words, "Only in the Lord" (1 Cor. 7:39).[3] Nowadays it seems as if people must be richer than they needed to be formerly before they set up house. It is a great pity that this should be so, for marriage is honorable in all, and it is not good for man to be alone, even though the young folks can afford to begin with only a "but and a ben."[4] Needless expense in show and furnishing is not confined to the rich.

A babe in a house is a wellspring of pleasure, and such new gifts from the Lord should call out our joyful sympathy. Let us remind our people of the solemnity of the vows they take upon themselves at the baptism of their children, and of the duty of paying these vows. We should try to deepen the impression felt at the dispensation of the ordinance. The Lord makes much use of family affliction in the training of his people, and cases of little children will often occur in an elder's district where the word is fulfilled, "Of such is the kingdom of heaven" (Matt. 19:14).

---

3. Here Dickson's point is that Christians may marry only other Christians.

4. According to the *Oxford English Dictionary* (Oxford University Press, 1933), "The words but and ben have special reference to the structure of dwelling houses formerly prevalent in the north, in which there was only one outer door, so that it was usual to enter through the kitchen, into the parlour, and through the latter to an inner chamber, bedroom, or the like."

Study Questions

1. How effectively do your session and congregation care for shut-ins and the sick? How can you improve the practical and spiritual care you provide for people suffering from illness?

2. List several ways in which God uses sickness to promote spiritual growth. How can elders help people gain the best spiritual advantage from grief and other trials?

3. What practical suggestions does Dickson make for effective visitation of the sick? Is there anything you would add? What are some "suitable books" to give to the sick?

4. How does your church help couples prepare for marriage? How can this aspect of your spiritual care be improved?

5. What does your church do to assist families with newborns? How do you help parents prepare for baptism? In what ways does your overall ministry to families need improvement?

7

FAMILY WORSHIP, THE YOUNG, INQUIRERS, SERVANTS

The elder will desire to have family worship established in all the households—so useful for domestic order, parental government, and family religion. Young people should be encouraged, when they settle in life, to resolve that wherever they have a house, God shall have an altar. He may give hints to those who already have family worship how to make it more interesting and useful to their young people, warning them against tediousness and formality, and suggesting such plans as, for example, the members of the family reading the verses in turn. And by kindly persuasion he may have an altar to God reared in families that have never yet called upon his name.

Extemporaneous prayer, even though it may be very short, is better than a read form; but when the heads of families feel that they cannot even do this, forms may be recommended.[1]

1. By "form," Dickson means a printed prayer, such as one might find in a devotional book or liturgical manual.

The elder may recommend also remembering in family prayer particular subjects at particular times, such as—for example—on Saturday morning ministers preparing for their Sabbath work, and the conversion of the Jews; on Sabbath morning, missionaries in foreign lands and Sabbath-school teachers and children.

Get them to sing praise as well as to read the Word and pray. It is sometimes complained that our Presbyterianism is too bald; don't let us make it unnecessarily so. "Happy is the people that know the joyful sound" (Ps. 89:15); and it adds more sunshine to family worship when they can all join in singing. Wherever there is a revival of religion, there is a revival of praise. Besides the cheerfulness that praise begets in a family, it may have a good influence on the neighbors; the sound of God's praise from a dwelling is to them as a flag for Christ. When he gave Paul and Silas songs in the night, "the prisoners heard them" (Acts 16:25). Philip Henry said that it was a way of exhibiting godliness, like Rahab's scarlet thread, to those who pass by our windows.[2]

Another important duty of the elder is taking an interest in the education of the children. If a family man, he may give useful hints even as to their weekly instruction; the schools they should attend, and their being kept at school as long as possible; the kind of books they should read; the choosing of good companions; etc. He should urge on parents the importance of making home happy and attractive so that, their father and mother being the children's most intimate friends, nothing may be kept from them, no bad habits formed, no bad books read in secret. Parents must take great pains with

2. Philip Henry (1631–1696) was the father of the well-known Puritan Bible commentator Matthew Henry.

their children; if they do not take trouble with them when young, they will give them trouble when they are old.

In the religious instruction of the children, however, the elder will feel it his duty to take a special interest. At baptism not only did the parents come under responsibility, but the church did so also. These baptized children are the children of the church, and as members of the visible church they must be taught. It was the command of our Lord that the lambs should be fed as well as the sheep. This has been too lightly thought of, and a handle has thus been given to opponents of infant baptism. By such means as the inculcating of parental instruction and the institution of classes for the children and young people of each congregation, the church of Christ must seek to do the duty that she undertook when she received these little ones into the fold of the visible church. She is not at liberty to make over her duty into the hands of parents, any more than *parents* are to throw over their responsibility on the *church*.

The elder will see that the children of his district are getting portions of the Word of God and the truths of the Shorter Catechism into their minds and hearts, and that they, as well as their parents, are regularly at church and understand the sermons. He should inquire as to their being at the congregational Sabbath school, which will depend much for its attendance upon what the minister and elders say about it; and it would be well, therefore, for him to visit it. Little books and tracts will be gladly received by the little ones, and he may give them out texts, psalms, or hymns to be repeated to him at his next visit. If there are many children in the district, he may occasionally have a meeting of them at his own house.

The young men and women in his district must be cared for too, those living both in families and in lodgings. An elder's influence over them as to their eternal interests, their choice of companions, and the formation of habits and acquaintanceships may be of lasting benefit. To the daughters leaving home as domestic servants, and to sons going forth among strangers, he should give words of warning and encouragement, with perhaps some little book suitable to their circumstances.

There is a tide in the affairs of souls—a time of impression. This is proved by the great number of conversions that take place between the ages of sixteen and twenty. Let the elder warn such young people against their peculiar temptations, for "Satan hath a friend at court in the heart of youth," and against the seductive influences of popery and ritualism, which spread their nets of music and sentimentality, trying to turn religion into one of the fine arts.[3] Childish they may be, but childish things are often powerful things. Above all, let him, in dependence on the Spirit's grace, seek to win the young to Jesus, that they may fix their choice forever on *him*, for then only they are safe. "May you be kept in Jesus!" said a friend of ours to a young convert. "Yes," he replied; "Jesus would not have *taken* me if he had not been able to *keep* me."

A word from a minister has much weight with all classes, for happily with us there is great respect for the office as well as for the individual. But a fitting word of counsel from an elder, kindly spoken, when felt to be from the heart, will touch a conscience that even a sermon cannot reach. While his office gives a weight to his words, yet his being on the same level somehow helps to send his words in between the joints of the

---

3. When he speaks of "popery," Dickson is referring to the Roman Catholic Church, and specifically to its earthly head, the Pope.

harness even more effectually than those of the minister; and this is true especially in the case of young men and women.

The promise is unto us and to *our children*. Even under the Old Testament there was special blessing in the covenant for them, and there is no less under the fuller, richer, and wider dispensation of the New. A mother once told me that the first thing that drew her heart to God was the *kindliness* of his covenant toward the children of believers. No doubt, under both dispensations salvation was and is of grace through actual personal faith in the case of those who reach years of understanding. Yet what precious encouragement there is for believing parents! And, as a matter of fact, we all know that the great proportion of additions to our churches are from the families of Christian parents. We must all have observed how often the passage from death unto life with such is almost imperceptible to those around them; and they usually become the steadiest and most intelligent members of the church. Should not Christian parents be more encouraged not only to hope and pray, but also confidently to expect that their children, whom they have dedicated to the Lord in baptism, shall all become his by converting grace?

Christian parents in these days may well be anxious about their children. The spirit of the age leads to a peculiar and precocious development of young people, and there is an earlier pressure from the world's tide of pleasure than formerly—"the lust of the flesh, the lust of the eye and the pride of life" (1 John 2:16). Passing along the street one day, I reproved a boy on seeing his unkindness to a child. "Who are *you?*" said he; "are you a policeman?" There is now more talk about *rights* than about *duties*, and parents too often obey their children, instead of children their parents. Of too many it may be said that they are "disobedient to parents" (Rom. 1:30), "heady and high-minded" (2 Tim. 3:4). Elders must remind parents as well as children that the Fifth Commandment has happily not been repealed; that parents must remember Eli (1 Sam. 3:13), and restrain as well as advise, while they avoid scolding and provoking their children to wrath (Eph. 6:4); that they must seek, especially by making home the happiest place to their children, to counterwork the enemy of souls, praying earnestly at the same time that they may be led to taste the joys of God's salvation, which will give them higher pleasures than theaters or ballrooms, and thus escape the corruption that is in the world through lust.

In the former days there was usually a certain severity on the part of fathers to their sons, who were led to fear and honor fully more than to love their parents, while in our days there is often too much indulgence and want of respect. Yet fathers should be specially advised to keep hold of their sons' affections by making them, from their earliest years, their most intimate friends and companions. "The bands of love are the cords of a man" (Hos. 11:4). A hard, iron rule is both unscriptural and unwise, and we see many examples of children being ruined by it even in Christian families.

Elders are often asked for hints as to making the Sabbath interesting and profitable to the young in a family. It is a difficult subject, as all parents know, for our children will never love the Sabbath as the "pearl of days" and as a spiritual privilege till they love the Lord of the Sabbath. Yet let not our children have cause to think it a gloomy day, for gloominess is not godliness, and sunshine is not sin. Let us surround the Sabbath in their minds with as many pleasant associations as possible. Let the restlessness of childhood find vent in variety of occupation, their curiosity in listening to Bible stories, their vivacity in the singing of hymns. It is well worthwhile for parents to give time and thought to this.

The habits and order of a Christian family will form a fence around the members of it when they go into the world. Let them be specially warned to shun bad companions and to avoid temptations as well as overcome them. Joseph "fled, and got him out" (Gen. 39:12). A young man, when departing for London, was advised never to go to a theater, never to go to races, never to travel on the Sabbath, never to play at cards. He strictly adhered to the advice, and after he became a new man he was often thankful for it. These four resolutions formed a valuable fence against temptation, and trained him to say *no* when sinners enticed him.

Our people should all know our dwelling, and feel that they are always welcome to come there when they wish to consult us. We may have visits from inquirers,[4] especially young men, whom we can often help very much. It will be well for them to feel that we can talk on other subjects besides religion and know other books besides our Bible. We can often be useful by lending them books; too many of these lie on our library shelves year after year that might be out at interest.

Especially let us welcome any anxious inquirers who may come to us, even though, as of old, secretly. In the minds of sincere and earnest young men there are often difficulties about doctrinal truths. If we see in them a humble and teachable spirit, let us beware of treating or denouncing them as heretics, which is very likely to make them such, and may scare them away from orthodoxy forever. The church has

---

4. What Dickson terms "inquirers" today are often called "seekers"— people who are interested in Christianity but have not yet come to Christ in faith and repentance.

been often a loser by conduct like this. Every doubt is not a skeptical doubt; it is often an honest intellectual difficulty. It would be well if some men had had more difficulties; they would be more firmly established than they seem to be, and not be so easily moved away after every will-o'-the-wisp that appears in the religious horizon. The grand system of our noble Confession of Faith is not to be taken on trust. It is only by studying the law and the testimony that we come to appreciate its truth. The more careful and prayerful study we give to it, the more, we believe, will the Confession of Faith be found in harmony with the Word of God. The danger to young men is in hasty, superficial study and self-confidence. We cannot take too many pains with a humble-minded and intelligent youth who comes to us with difficulties about doctrinal truths; and he will often go to an elder sooner than to a minister. When he does understand the way of God more perfectly, he will be more useful than a dozen men who have adopted the Confession because their ministers or their fathers did so, and not because it has passed through the crucible of their own minds and souls.

In the instruction and examination of young communicants the elder may much assist the minister.[5] How important is this crisis? It can never occur again. Our first communion! Do we not all remember it? What an opportunity given for earnest dealing with the soul! How important that the profession be genuine and, next in importance, that those who have set their faces Zionward be guided aright, for a minister's and an elder's oversight is specially needed then!

5. Communicants are the children of church members who have made a public profession of faith and thus are eligible to receive the sacrament of the Lord's Supper.

Their care does not cease at the conversion of one of their people. The unsteady walk of many believers may often be traced to their having got a wrong *set*, as it were, at the beginning of their religious life. The necessity for solid spiritual food and for much prayer and study of the Word may not have been impressed on them, and hence a liking for excitement and novelties, resembling the state of appetite that can live only on dainties and sweetmeats.

An elder can also do much in guiding a young convert, especially as to his daily life—more in some respects than the minister, who can, of course, know little of the conflicts of grace in the workshop or the place of business. The young disciple must learn to stand the tear and wear of contact with men of all kinds, and he needs grace to enable him to stand his ground and "adorn the doctrine of God his Savior" (Titus 2:10). Strange stories have we heard; how many martyrdoms are gone through in these days of great liberality! The jests of scoffers are hard to bear,

> For ridicule will oftentimes prevail,
> And cut the knot when graver reasons fail.

The sneer of a silly maid overcame the strength of him who said, "If I should die with thee, yet I will not deny thee" (Matt. 26:35). To *live* for Christ is to many more difficult than it would be to *die* for him. Yet those who will live godly in the world shall suffer persecution (2 Tim. 3:12). Perhaps companionship in one's duties with a mere formalist, one who has not heart-religion, is still more dangerous to a warm young convert. As a support against such temptations let him think how much good he may do by simply leading a consistent Christian life. A friend who well knew infidels and their mode of attack told me that there was one argument that an infidel could never meet—the morality taught by Jesus Christ. The young disciple cannot, perhaps, argue well with his mouth, but let him by his life manifest the spirit of Jesus, "showing out of a good conversation his works with meekness of wisdom" (James 3:13); let him show that faith in Jesus makes a man a better servant, a more faithful clerk, and a kinder friend.

At the admission of young communicants it has been found in some cases useful that, besides the address by the minister, one or two elders should add a few words, referring, perhaps, to their own feelings at their first communion, and setting before the new members of the church the dangers they may be exposed to, with a few words of practical direction and encouragement. The mouths of two or three witnesses may be useful at such a time.

"I have growing hopes that every child of mine is a child of God, and every servant of mine is a servant of Christ." So writes one who, as the head of a large family, desired to "command his children and his household after him to keep the way of the LORD" (Gen. 18:19).

It is the duty of every master and mistress to care for the souls of their servants[6]—to give them religious instruction as part of their own family. It is often difficult for an elder to take proper oversight of them. They do not live in their own house, and their time belongs to their master and mistress. Many domestic servants change their places too often, never seeming to take root in any one family. "Why do you wish to

6. Dickson was writing at a time when upper- and even middle-class families had domestic servants. His comments here would apply to family life and to any work situation in which a Christian has spiritual authority over others.

leave?" is often a question asked by a mistress of a servant who proposes to give up her place. "I have been very happy here, and you have been very kind to me; but I just think I have been long enough in one place," is the not unusual reply. Servants are a large and important class, on which the comfort of households largely depends. Elders are too apt to take for granted the difficulty of visiting them. We have known many cases in which careful provision was made by mistresses for the elder's visit to their servants, while no doubt in other cases there is difficulty in getting access to them. If the elder is blessed with a good and prudent wife, she may assist him much in this as in other departments of his work. She may call on the servants, and invite them to come to his house at a time convenient for both.

If there are many servants in his district, he may have a meeting for them all, on either a weekday or Sabbath evening, when he can speak to them as Paul told Titus to do, cautioning them against temptations, exhorting them to adorn the doctrine of God their Savior, and showing how they may do it (see Titus 2:10). Classes for female servants may do much good, provided that the place of meeting is not far distant from their homes and there is communication between the teacher and the mistresses, so as to ensure the actual attendance of the servants. A very safe and useful plan is for a lady to form a class for the servants in a particular street, square, or locality.

Christian servants may, like the Syrian maid (2 Kings 5:1–4), be a blessing to their employers, to their fellow servants, and to the children of the family. Through them salvation has often come to a house. We know of at least two eminently useful Christians in our day who ascribe their first serious impressions to domestics—one to the early lessons of his nurse, the other to the words of a laundry-maid in the family.

Study Questions

1. What are the essential elements of family worship? Why is family worship important to the health of the family? Of the church?

2. How does your church teach fathers and mothers to lead in family worship? What musical, devotional, catechetical, and instructional resources do you recommend?

3. In what ways does your church fulfill its task of providing biblical and theological instruction for children? How can elders promote the spiritual growth of children in the church?

4. How does your church care for young people who are making the transition into adulthood? How do you reach out to college students, both while they are at home and while they are away at school? What encouragement do you give to students entering the work force? What practical steps do you need to take in order to improve in these areas of ministry?

5. Dickson emphasizes the importance of reaching young people with the gospel. Evaluate your own practice and effectiveness in personal evangelism, especially with young people. List several ways in which this aspect of your ministry needs to improve.

6. What are the most difficult challenges that young people face in our culture? What is the role of the elder in helping young people develop a healthy attitude toward authority? What are some ways that elders can help young people build what Dickson describes as "fences" against temptation?

7. Dickson advocates a balance between severity and indulgence in the fatherly training of sons. How does a father reach a son's heart?

8. How are you making the Sabbath a delight (Isa. 58:13)? How are you encouraging other members of the church to do the same?

9. Dickson speaks of "inquirers." Today they are often called "seekers": people who are interested enough in religion to attend church, but are still evaluating the claims of Christ. What can elders do to help seekers find Christ? As a church and as an individual Christian, how are you showing hospitality to people who have not yet made their home with God?

10. Describe some ways in which an elder can help someone with spiritual doubts.

11. What plan does your church have for the instruction, examination, and discipleship of children who are ready to become communicants? Are the young people in your church growing in Christ? What can be done to promote their spiritual vitality?

12. In what ways is it appropriate for an elder's wife to assist her husband in his spiritual work? If you are married, what are you doing to promote your wife's long-term spiritual growth and fruitfulness in ministry?

8

SPECIAL MEANS OF DOING GOOD

District prayer meetings have often been found a means of grace. It is best to have them weekly; fortnightly or monthly meetings have seldom been found to thrive well. Where there is a weekly congregational prayer meeting, district ones, unless at a distance from the church, are not usually well attended. They may be for one district alone, or two districts may be combined, the two elders taking part in them, with the help of the deacons and some of the people. In some, reading of the Word is accompanied with a short exposition; in others, along with the reading of the Word there is given interesting missionary intelligence or extracts fitted to be useful. Praise, heartily sung in suitable psalms or hymns, is both pleasant and profitable. Cases of distress in the district should be specially remembered, the names of the afflicted being mentioned as in a family. The meetings should rarely exceed one hour in length. As regards the place, private houses are found to be not so convenient as a schoolroom, the session house, or the hall that should be attached to every church.

The minister should be invited to visit these meetings occasionally. Where there can be no regular district meetings, the elder may hold one occasionally—before each communion, for example. Some elders have the gift of conducting such meetings in an edifying and interesting way—others have not; we can use only what gifts we have. However desirable, therefore, these meetings should not in all cases be considered as part of the duty lying on an elder in the same sense as regular visitation is.

If circumstances permit it, an elder will find it pleasant and profitable to occasionally have his people at a tea meeting in his house. It makes them better acquainted with each other, and the time may be spent very usefully.

In a country village of which we know, there has been a prayer meeting conducted now for more than a hundred years. That place has been blessed three or four times with a revival of religion—shall we not say in answer to these prayers? This interesting fact was also told us: that when the tide of blessing was about to come in, the numbers began unaccountably to increase till the place was too strait for them; even outside the door there were many earnest attenders. The people knew that the tide was far out when the number fell to five or six. Then they began to pray again for a turning of the tide, and a spring tide came. Alas! in many of our congregations the tide is far out, if we are to judge by attendance at prayer meetings, which are a kind of gauge of spiritual life; yet let those who attend them continue to pray on. We would urge also the importance of keeping open such wells of salvation as prayer meetings and weekly sermons, even though few may come to them. They are places to which thirsting and anxious ones repair, and we are not always to judge of their usefulness by the numbers that come.

In every way let an elder seek to stir up his people to pray—private prayer especially, but social also. Prayer is the most practical and powerful thing in the world, for it moves the Hand that moves the universe.

He should encourage as much as possible the formation and lively continuance of fellowship meetings. These are not so common now as formerly, for religion has got in our times into more public developments—whether for more personal edification or not is doubtful. Five or six members of the congregation who are neighbors may be encouraged to meet together. There may be meetings for men, and others for women—the former in the evening, the latter in the middle of the day—once a week, for an hour or even less. The mothers in the district might be encouraged to meet for prayer for their children. "Then they that feared the LORD spake often one to another; and the Lord hearkened and heard it" (Mal. 3:16). As John Bunyan says:

> Saints' fellowship, if it be managed well,
> Will keep us alive, and that in spite of hell.[1]

Many years ago one of my people, a poor bedridden woman (an old servant of Dr. Andrew Thomson of St. George's),[2] used to spend the time of each church service in

---

1. The English nonconformist John Bunyan (1628–1688) was imprisoned for twelve years for preaching without state approval. He is best remembered as the author of *The Pilgrim's Progress* (1678) and *Grace Abounding to the Chief of Sinners* (1666).

2. Andrew Thomson (1779–1831) was a significant Church of Scotland leader and preacher at St. George's, Edinburgh. As editor of the *Edinburgh Christian Instructor* and as an active member of both presbytery and General Assembly, he had considerable influence within the church and the state.

praying for the Spirit's blessing on the Word being preached to our congregation. It was a means of grace to sit by that bedside. One day when I called, I learned that that morning she had been suddenly called up to be with Jesus. To her it was far better, but as a few devout men carried her to her lowly tomb at Warriston, they thought she was one who could be ill spared; she had lived so as to be missed.

Your district of fifteen or twenty families is a little world, or rather a church in miniature. There are all ages—the little children, the young men, the fathers. And there are all varieties of temper and disposition and spiritual state—the careless, those at ease in Zion, the anxious, the newborn believer, the fretful, the desponding, the lively, the peaceful, the rejoicing, the steady, the excitable, those who have left their first love, and those who are pressing toward the mark. There are Peters and Thomases, Marys and Marthas, Pliables and Stand-fasts, Little Faiths and Great Hearts; and among them all there is a constant change going on.[3] Your one specific for all cases is, "Looking unto Jesus" (Heb. 12:2). For saints and sinners, he is the one thing needful. For ourselves and for our people, the balm of Gilead and the living Physician are our all in all. Looking to him, we are lightened, we are humbled, we are sanctified, changed into his image "from glory to glory" (2 Cor. 3:18), "the peace of God, which passeth all understanding, keeping our hearts and minds" (Phil. 4:7).

An elder must be instant in season and out of season, watching for opportunities of doing good among his people. We have referred to times of affliction, when his visits will be warmly welcomed. But if he is absent from home at the time,

3. The names in this sentence denote people from the Bible and characters in Bunyan's famous allegory, *The Pilgrim's Progress* (1678).

he may send a letter to the afflicted. This suggestion occurs to me from my having found that some such letters of a former generation had been carefully preserved and made useful to children and grandchildren long after writer and receiver had gone to the better country. Even though we are not [away] from home we may find it useful, in peculiar circumstances, to write letters to some of our people. They are more lasting than any words of counsel casually given.

The New Year, as already remarked, is a time when we should especially remember our people. For the last twenty years I have been in the practice of sending at that time to each member or family a packet containing one or two carefully selected tracts, which I considered likely to be most profitable to the individual case. It is a very small New Year's gift, to be sure, but it is a token of remembrance, and has always been kindly received. Little books may be substituted for tracts, and something may also be sent to the children. At that season there is always a supply of useful and interesting publications. The poorer members should be considered at that time, and to them our packet may be accompanied with more substantial gifts if the elder has it easily in his power to give them. For the aged poor I have found a little good tea by far the most acceptable gift of the kind.

With reference to books that we may give to our people or others, whether old or young, I will venture to offer a few hints. They need not be large or expensive, but they must be readable. No sermon can do any good unless it is heard, for faith comes by hearing; so books can do good only if read, and to be read they must be readable and interesting, not dry or prosy. Narratives and biographies are usually the best to give away, unless there is such spiritual appetite and intelligence as will appreciate and profit by books of a deeper kind.

Books and tracts in very small type should be avoided; visibility is indispensable. Narratives are always to be preferred, and if illustrated, so much the better for both old and young. Children like stories and pictures, and we are all but grown-up children.

As a rule, we should not give away books that have not been read by ourselves or by others on whose judgment we can rely. If, however, I had to hastily select books or tracts for this purpose, I would take as tests of their being interesting and readable that they were narrative, illustrated, in good type, with short paragraphs, and with many proper names. When we give a book to anyone, we should put on it the name of the giver and receiver, adding a short text [i.e., a Bible verse] written out. Lastly, and most important of all, let us follow every book we give with prayer, that the blessing of God may go with it.

When our people leave us for another part of the country or for a distant place, we should not be satisfied merely with their taking with them certificates of church membership, but we should try, for some time at least, to keep up a link of connection with them by an occasional letter, newspaper, or book. We find that they value these very much when far away, and not least any printed congregational lists or reports. It is a great help to a young man in a distant place to know that at least one old friend is still interested in him. When our members or adherents remove to a distance, let us try to get someone in the place to which they have gone to give them a welcome there. If we have no friend there, we may recommend them to the kindness of the minister of the place, or to the young men's associations that exist in most of our leading towns. Letters of introduction are good, but unfortunately they are not always delivered; we should, in addition to giving these, write directly, if possible, to someone in the place. A youth in a foreign land once explained how he was brought to the Savior by saying, "My Sabbath-school teacher at home never forgot me." Let elders, as far as they can, do likewise.

In large towns there is a constant influx of young men from the rural districts and smaller towns. Many of these are the most active and intelligent of their class. I often sympathize with ministers who have thus to part with the most promising fruits of their ministry just when beginning to be useful. These classes of youths should be cared for on their arrival. Our larger congregations should make provision for this. Scarcely a winter passes without hearing of sad cases where youths, from the want of someone to care for them, have been sucked into the whirlpool of city dissipation, and have had to be sent home with empty purse, broken character, and ruined health. There are many shipwrecks at sea, but, alas! there are many shipwrecks on shore too. Our young men are often very friendless and lonely, and the change from home family life to living in lodgings is depressing enough, and to young men of very social dispositions is often dangerous. Ministers cannot be expected to undertake this work. It should be considered the business of one or two elders in each congregation to welcome any young men who come about the church, introducing them to the Bible class, the young men's society, and similar good influences, besides occasionally inviting them to their own houses if circumstances permit. Cases often occur, too, where, from want of attention to regular and sufficient diet and other indispensables to good health, earnest students sow the seeds of premature death or lifelong debility. Elders and elders' wives may take a kindly interest in such cases. A few words of timely counsel may save a useful life. Through their efforts the anxieties of many a father and mother would be relieved and their prayers answered.

Elders of districts that contain many persons in humble life will find great benefit from having, besides the aid of the deacon, the help and cooperation of a female visitor. Many ladies who could not undertake ordinary district-visiting among the poor could discharge this duty. A woman's eye and heart and her knowledge of details enable her to suggest modes of giving help that would never occur to a man. This applies especially to cases of sickness and poverty. A large amount of labor is expended on the poor outside the church—often on the vicious and improvident poor. We do not regret this, but the poor members of our churches should share more largely than we think they do in that affectionate and long-suffering persistency that is shown by Christian women in caring for individuals. Christ's own poor have been given over by him to the care of his church, and in this respect his disciples should try to set their feet in the footprints of him who has left them an example (1 Peter 2:21). Many of his poor have a sore struggle against poverty—as they often themselves express it, "they have a *sair fecht* [sore fight]" to get through—and through much care and anxiety, many of them do enter the kingdom (Acts 14:22).

Cases occur of great delicacy and difficulty, and in dealing with them the elder must take care to give no occasion for his good being evil spoken of. He will find it useful in dealing with women, either old or young, to have the advice and help of his wife or some other Christian woman of sense and experience.

Elders of the church should be men ready for every good work—ready to distribute, willing to communicate. To every cry for help, whether for the bodies or the souls of men, we should instinctively be disposed to say *yes*, rather than *no*. It will help Christ's cause in the world if we can lend a helping hand to the many charities that exist among us. Christ was the real Founder of them all. Their very names remind us of him, who was the first friend of the destitute sick, the orphan, the blind, the incurables, and the deaf and dumb. Such charities can be best managed by those who are in sympathy with their Founder.

While each one cannot take an active interest in *every* good work—for concentration of personal effort is necessary—yet we can help, as far as our means allow, with our subscriptions as well as our sympathy and prayers.[4] We rejoice to think that the practical management of the various charities, as anyone may see from their reports, is largely in the hands of the elders of the various churches. Let it continue to be so, for they will thus show the world that none will feel or care much for either its sins or sorrows but those who have learned from Jesus to do so.

Elders should also be ready to take their share in municipal and other public work. Such duties are often irksome, yet of immense usefulness, and the best men in each community should be called to them.

Those elders who have gifts for evangelistic work should be willing to engage in it, for people listen with peculiar interest and attention to an unprofessional witness for Christ. This makes even a few stammering words from a layman sometimes weighty and useful. I was standing one evening beside my old friend Robert Flockhart, the good old soldier who preached at the west corner of St. Giles' Church, Edinburgh, every night for forty years. A scoffer came up and listened

---

4. By "subscriptions" Dickson means pledges or financial contributions to Christian charities.

for a few moments, when he indignantly exclaimed to me, "Men like that do more harm than ministers, for nobody can say *he* is paid for his preaching." While we do not labor in Word or doctrine, we should be ready, according to our ability, to speak for him of whose love we have tasted. Now that most of our elders have been Sabbath-school teachers, we should have a large number of them able and willing to take part in evangelistic meetings either in mission halls or at open-air services. To be able to give short addresses and to lead in singing praise is well worth some time spent in self-training. If our ministers had a large staff of well-educated and earnest elders at their disposal, they would be encouraged to use churches and mission rooms much more frequently than at present for weekday and special services.

Holidays are now a universal institution for old as well as young, and every summer many city elders spend a month or six weeks in the country. Let us try to make these visits to the country not only pleasant and health-giving, but to some extent useful and profitable. We have known of a church built and a congregation gathered through the two months' sojourn of an earnest elder. We do not expect often to find such a result from a holiday, for holidays should be holidays and not be devoted to hard work, especially in the case of men who work with their brains all the rest of the year. Fresh air, fresh scenery, and quiet are what they require, for both their bodies and their brains.

Yet a Christian elder will try to do good wherever he goes. It will be no trouble to him, for it is his life, his joy, to be ever about his Father's business. Coming as a stranger into a country town or village, there are many little ways in which he can help on the cause of Christ, and encourage those who have little of the excitement and sympathy that help those of us who live in large towns; for how much do we owe to the impulse of others!

He should, for example, regularly attend the church in the place, if there is one, connected with his own denomination. It is discouraging to a minister in the country to find visitors whom he reasonably expects to wait on his ministry wandering away to another. Besides regular Sabbath attendance on the minister of our own church, let our sympathies and influence be used to strengthen his hands. Many a faithful minister is laboring on in a quiet sphere from year to year in faith, yet under many difficulties and discouragements. The educated Christian people in his congregation, to whom he can speak his whole heart, may be but few in number, and by sympathy and encouragement we may be able to cheer him in his work and send him on his way rejoicing.

We say from experience that any service that an elder, while in the country, may be able to render will be very cordially welcomed, such as taking part in the weekly prayer meeting or assisting in the Sabbath school, the Bible class, or the teachers' meeting. He will often receive as well as give. He will often get practical hints from country ministers and country congregations that never occurred to him before, and that he can make use of when he returns home. At the same time, he will find that any hints he can give from his town experience, as to either the temporal or spiritual matters connected with congregational work, will be gladly received, and acted upon if suited to the circumstances of the locality or congregation.

There are two kinds of work that we have always felt peculiar pleasure in. One of these is the visiting of sick people. Sometimes ministers feel debarred by a feeling of delicacy from visiting sick people connected with churches other than their own. But a Christian visitor may go where he likes, and he is always welcomed. Often a blessing follows a word spoken in Christ's name when a stranger brings it.

When packing our baggage for the country, let us not forget a large bundle of good tracts—narrative ones, if possible, and if with a woodcut at the beginning so much the better.[5] Little colored tracts for children must also be included, and a good supply of the pretty Sabbath-school papers; and let there be a great plenty of these, for we may unexpectedly have a run upon our bank and be left tractless. We happened one day to be passing along the road when a large country school was dispersing, and we could not supply the eager demand of the youngsters for tracts.

It may happen that in the place of our temporary sojourn the different ministers and people do not work very cordially together. A visitor, if he is a man of good sense and a lover of all good men, can do much to smooth away difference. All the more that he is a stranger is he able to be a mediator and reconciler. And he can best do this not by probing into old sores and trying to settle old disagreements, but with genial Christian kindliness leading brethren who have been for a time estranged to engage together in some good work. It is not so much by discussing the nature and duty of Christian union that we can do good in such cases, as by drawing out into exercise the brotherly love that, though it may lie deep down, certainly does exist in every sanctified heart.

5. A woodcut is a pictorial design cut into a wooden block and then printed, in this case on the cover of a booklet.

"The sweetest surprisals of eternity," wrote Dr. James Hamilton, "will be resurrections of the works of time. When the disciple has forgotten the labor of love he will be reminded of it in the rich reward. To find the marvelous results which have accrued from feeble means, to find the prosperous fruit already growing on the shores of eternity from seeds which you scattered on the stream of time, will augment the exceeding weight of glory" (cf. 2 Cor. 4:17).[6]

6. James Hamilton (1814–1867) served as minister of the National Scotch Church in London from 1841 to his death, and also as the editor of *Presbyterian Messenger and Evangelical Christendom*.

Study Questions

1. What are the essential elements of a healthy small group? How are small groups in your church established, organized, and supervised? How are small-group leaders trained? What is the role of elders in your small-group structure?

2. What is the connection between the vitality of small groups and the overall spiritual health of the church? Using this standard, evaluate the health of your church.

3. Dickson describes prayer meetings as "a kind of gauge of spiritual life." Using this standard, evaluate the prayer life of your congregation. What can elders do to encourage God's people to pray?

4. Dickson advocates the use of "fellowship meetings"—gatherings of Christians who share a similar situation in life (men, women, singles, students, youth, etc.). What meetings like this does your church sponsor? What meetings are needed?

What is the proper role of elders in promoting this kind of fellowship?

5. List the various spiritual needs of the people who are under your spiritual care. What help do they need? What are some practical ways in which you can maintain personal contact with them throughout the week?

6. How does your church say farewell to people who are moving away from the congregation? How can elders help ensure that those who leave find new church homes and maintain their spiritual vitality?

7. What is the role of the elder in helping newcomers get integrated into the spiritual life of the church?

8. Dickson mentions the value of "female visitors." What is your church doing to promote the use of women's gifts for ministry? In what ways can women properly assist the elders in their work? What safeguards are in place to ensure that your elders maintain suitable boundaries of propriety in their spiritual care for women?

9. Elders should lead by example in charity, in society, and in evangelism. Evaluate your own involvement in charitable, civic, and evangelistic causes. How effectively are you serving God in the world? Are there any areas of responsibility that you are neglecting?

10. What are some ways in which you can make good spiritual use of your vacation time?

9

CASES OF DISCIPLINE

Dealing with cases of discipline is the most painful—indeed, the only painful—duty an elder has to discharge. Offenses, however, will come, and melancholy and saddening they often are, for fleshly lusts still war against the soul (1 Peter 2:11). Alas! all churches have cause to lie low before God on this account. "But I keep under my body, and bring it into subjection, lest that by any means when I have preached to others, I myself may be a castaway" (1 Cor. 9:27); "Wherefore, let him that thinketh he standeth take heed lest he fall" (1 Cor. 10:12) are words of warning much needed by ourselves, and that come anew with a solemn emphasis in cases coming before a church session. For the right discharge of the duty of discipline the elder requires the spirit both of faithfulness and of tenderness. These are fully illustrated in our Lord's dealings with offenders, which we should often study. How faithful was he, and yet how tender! Oh, that we could deal with erring brethren in the spirit of Jesus Christ!

The first and great end of discipline, as laid down in Scripture, is the restoration and salvation of the offender. The second is the maintaining of the purity of the church and freeing it from scandal. The first object must ever be kept prominent. With all respect for our forefathers, it has often occurred to me that they were too apt to overlook this. I have looked over a good many old session records, and they suggested too much the idea of the elder as a kind of ecclesiastical patrol, turning his bull's-eye upon the spots and blemishes in church members. Our criminal code was then written without and within with blood; and in days when a boy could be executed for stealing five shillings, without even a remonstrance from the Christian heart of the country, it is not wonderful that our church discipline was tinged with severity. No doubt records and minutes are cold and formal things; they don't give us a photograph of the meetings of session; they don't record the faltering voice or the tearful eye with which the detailed reports were received and the discipline exercised. As some of them read, they don't seem to breathe the spirit of the Christian dispensation. This mistake as to the chief end of discipline has not been long extinct. It is not yet forty years since an aged acquaintance of mine, in delicate health at the time, chose on a wet Sabbath afternoon to go to a church at her door instead of her own at a distance. For this offense she was taken under discipline and was cut off from church-fellowship.

An elder should be very cautious how he listens to evil reports against a member of the church. If he encourages tittle-tattle of this kind, he will hear plenty of it, to his own vexation. But if a report reaches him that has an apparent look of truth about it, or if he has himself seen anything calling for action on his part, he should lose no time in making inquiry in a private and prudent way. First speak to your brother alone, and deal with him faithfully and kindly. Be straightforward and candid. Avoid roundabout ways of opening the subject, as if you had called about some other business. Be in no hurry to bring the matter before the session if there is no public scandal, and always consult with your minister before doing so. Every effort must be made by you privately, in the spirit of the words, "I now tell you even weeping" (Phil. 3:18), and you may gain your brother (Matt. 18:15). I have heard from elders of many cases where a manifest blessing followed discipline, though these cases never reached the session. When a case comes before the session, as it ought to do if it has caused scandal, two of the brethren are usually appointed to wait on the offender.[1] The less formality and publicity, at least at first, the better. The supposed publicity and notoriety of sessional dealing is against the hope of penitence because of its irritation to an offender; and there should be no delay, for that may give him a pillow for his conscience, as if he had not gotten full justice. Avoid coldness, harshness, or denunciation in your dealings. These are not likely to do any good, and do not come well from a fellow sinner saved by grace who acts as a servant and representative of Jesus. Let us beware of the idea, so apt to creep into our minds in such circumstances, that if we are just faithful enough we have at least delivered our own soul. No; we do this only when we have prayerfully and humbly done all that we can to bring our erring brother to the feet of Jesus.

The experience of ministers and elders has often been expressed to the effect that the ordinance of discipline, rightly conducted, is frequently blessed as a means of grace, and that in cases where the discipline is both of a private and of a public kind.

---

1. Dickson is describing what in today's nomenclature would be termed a "commission" of session.

Every elder is himself in danger of backsliding, and so are his people. Watching over this is part of his duty as appointed to feed the flock (literally, to tend them like a shepherd), and it is required of him that he be found faithful in this. Watch the beginnings of evil, like the letting out of water. Your knowledge of each, and your daily intercourse with all classes of men, will make you of quick understanding as to the sin likely to beset each of your little flock. There are abounding temptations, especially among the working classes, in our large towns. There are far too many public houses: we say "far too many" as an opinion in which all must agree, for we do not here advocate extreme views, although we can well sympathize with them.[2] How much hopeful good do they destroy! How many buds of early promise do they wither! How like a spider's web they often are in a district! Every faithful elder and missionary sorrowfully knows that there are far too many "licensed" enemies of his work. We speak, of course, of the system, not of individuals—a system that instinctively seems to ally itself with all evil influences.

---

2. A "public house" is a pub—a bar or tavern. Although Dickson was not a teetotaler, he lamented the prevalence of such establishments in the towns and cities of Scotland.

Study Questions

1. Give several examples of how Jesus dealt with people who broke God's law. What aspects of his holy character are most helpful for elders in the proper exercise of church discipline?

2. What are the primary goals of church discipline?

3. What spirit should elders display as they exercise church discipline? What happens when elders fail to show this kind of godliness?

4. List and describe the basic steps in the biblical process of church discipline.

5. How effective is your session in carrying out church discipline? Evaluate your goals for discipline, your attitude toward people who need it, and your adherence to the biblical process.

6. How well do the members of your congregation understand the value, purpose, and proper exercise of church discipline? What is your session doing to educate the congregation on this subject?

10

MEMBERS ENCOURAGED TO WORK

We must try to get all the members of the church practically interested in the work of Christ, for "none of us liveth to himself" (Rom. 14:7). It was said of a colt, "The Lord hath need of him" (Mark 11:3). Much more may this be said of those who profess to be living members of Christ's body. What each should do will depend on what each can do, for "she hath done what she could" was the Master's word of approval (Mark 14:8). "As we have opportunity" is the rule laid down for us (Gal. 6:10). What a change would appear on the church and the world if each professing Christian were doing something—something for Christ—even though it were a very little! Might not the wilderness soon be turned into a fruitful field?

Attention to personal religion, regular reading of the Word, and prayer is the first duty. This, with the care of a family and conscientious attention to business, will leave to many of our people little time for duties outside. A mother may adorn the doctrine more by her care of her husband and children, and by keeping a tidy and well-ordered house, than if she neglected these and engaged in visitation or teaching the poor. Home is her first sphere, and a more useful one she cannot find. It is wonderful how much some mothers can do by activity and method with a willing heart. Yet other things must be done only after home duties. What a field of usefulness is the family! Richer and brighter sheaves are not to be found in God's harvest than can be gathered in by a praying mother. It is well for the elder to keep this in view, and not to seem to underrate home duties. The husband or sons should be encouraged in their lawful callings, and an elder is often able to give practical help as well as encouragement in these.

Let us engage the hearts of our people in the cause of missions at home and abroad. Alas! How little do the perishing heathen lie as a burden on our hearts! How little is given to foreign missions in comparison with what is spent on ourselves at home—our houses, our furniture, our gardens, our recreations! The missionary cause is the church's great work, but it is also the work of every individual member of it. It is the duty of an elder very specially to remind his people of this. "The harvest truly is plenteous, but the laborers are few. Pray ye therefore the Lord of the harvest that he would send forth laborers into his harvest" (Matt. 9:37–38). This is the world's harvest, and all must be busy in harvest time. Cases have been known where the first impulse given to the young missionary has come from the elder of his district. Our people should feel that this subject is near our hearts. Let us often speak of it to them; and it might increase their daily interest in it if we gave each family a missionary box, into which there might be put occasional thank offerings for family mercies received. Let me commend to elders, for their own profit and that of their people, Dr. James Hamilton's tract *Thankfulness*, the sermon he preached to the Wesleyan Missionary Society.[1] It was, we know, his own favorite of all his writings, and one that has been much blessed.

Members of the church who have not many home duties, and who are eager to do good, should be invited and encouraged to engage in such work as visiting the poor, teaching in the Sabbath school, collecting for the various funds of the church, or distributing tracts, assisting at mothers' meetings, Dorcas meetings, psalmody classes, etc. You may thus be honored to set some to work who will be far more useful than you have ever been. I have found good results to follow from taking young people to see well-conducted Sabbath schools and other Christian agencies at work. This tends to develop any desire in them for usefulness, and enables us to give them practical hints that may be of lasting value. When Dr. Nettleton was a young man, he got this advice: "Do all the good you can in the world, and make as little noise about it as possible."[2] This maxim, he says, had ever afterward great influence upon him. Given to him when his mind was very impressionable, it became a rule of his conduct all through his singularly useful life.

It is usually best when young people begin to work that it be in connection with their own congregation. It will be more under the elder's eye, and young and timid people will

1. James Hamilton, *Thankfulness* (1850).
2. Asahel Nettleton (1783–1844) was a Connecticut Congregational evangelist during the Second Great Awakening (1787–1825), when his Calvinist preaching—in strong opposition to the Arminian methods of the revivalist Charles Finney (1792–1875)—was instrumental in the conversion of thousands.

be encouraged by the sight of well-known faces. They will get acquainted with other working members of the church with whom they may have Christian fellowship, and be kept from a good many dangers that beset those who take up work at their own hand. Plymouthists and other sectaries are ever hovering around movements outside the church, eager to proselytize for their little sects the young and ardent disciples.[3] The more simple and private kinds of work are always the safest, especially for beginners. Train them to work by faith, and not by sight, so that they will have a motive superior to external discouragements. Don't urge any to engage in many things at once. It may distract and over-burden them, and may lead to their giving up such work altogether. And let elders warn young men against neglecting their ordinary business or giving it but a secondary place in their thoughts. An employer once complained to me that he found a clerk studying his Sabbath-school lesson instead of writing his ledger. This ought not to be; "not slothful in business" must go along with "fervent in spirit" (Rom. 12:11). An experienced friend said to me, "If a man is not good at his own business, neither the church nor the world will be the better for him."

Let elders impress on their people that their daily commonplace duties may become a means of grace to them, their daily mercies, trials, and anxieties a means of fellowship with Jesus—that he should be linked with every detail of their

---

3. The "Plymouthists," as Dickson calls them, are more usually known as the Plymouth Brethren. Among their distinctive views is the denial of the office of elder, whether teaching or ruling. Other denominations and sects were also growing rapidly in Scotland after the 1830s, and Dickson wanted to protect young Presbyterians from their advances.

daily life by their "telling Jesus" everything, casting every burden on the Lord, all their care on him (1 Peter 5:7).

And let them further remind them that, while they may and should become sowers of the precious seed of the Word in the Sabbath school or elsewhere, they should remember that they have a sphere that none but themselves can occupy, in their own families, in their places of business, and among their acquaintances. Let them seek the spiritual good of those with whom they come daily in contact. Their lives as well as their lips should be scented with the sweet smell of the Rose of Sharon (Song 2:1). As mechanics, clerks, masters, mistresses, servants, teachers, governesses, they should repeat and illustrate the good lessons of the Sabbath by being living epistles all through the busy week from the Monday morning till the Saturday night.

The domestic history of the church of Christ in former days is not abundant. One can understand the reasons for this, and also how in our day, when of making books there is no end, the want should be so much greater. But to one who has at all gone back on the past, it is a very striking circumstance that the earnest effort that was formerly directed to the conversion of brothers and sisters, of friends and companions, now finds vent in the Sabbath school, and even in more public means of usefulness. We ought all to remember that the sphere of duty nearest to us must ever be first attended to. That must be done, while we should not leave the other undone.

As further reason for elders stirring up their people to good works, it should not be forgotten that Christians derive much spiritual health and blessing from efforts to do good to others. Exercise is indispensable for sound health of either body or soul. Elders must all have observed that one who has been brooding over his soul's maladies receives good from the fresh air and exercise got in working for Christ. Many have felt it to be like life from the dead to be drawn away from the morbid feeling of their own spiritual pulse to teaching little children the simple story of the cross. To be occupied with our little selves is not God's way of making us either healthy or happy.

Study Questions

1. How involved are the members of your church in Christian work? List several ways that elders can help get church members interested in the work of Christ—personally, locally, and nationally.

2. Dickson warns us not to "underrate home duties." What can elders do to encourage wives and mothers in their domestic duties?

3. Evaluate the overall strength of your missions program. How engaged is the congregation in prayer? How generous are your people in giving to missionary work? Who is being trained and sent out as missionaries? How can elders help church members get more personally involved in the global work of the gospel?

4. What are some ways that people can do the Lord's work through your church? How can you most effectively recruit and train people for service, according to their spiritual gifts?

5. How does your church train young people for ministry? What are some practical ways that this aspect of your ministry can grow?

6. Why is it important for Christians to be good workers? How does our daily work help us to grow in grace? In what ways are you "telling Jesus" in the details of your daily work?

7. List several ways that Christians can do spiritual good at home, at work, and with their friends. How do good works promote our spiritual growth?

11

FELLOWSHIP AMONG CHURCH MEMBERS

One great evil existing in our congregations, especially in large towns, is that many of the members do not know or take an interest in each other. It is a blessed hope that we shall recognize our friends in heaven, but let us begin by first recognizing them on earth. We have actually heard of people living in the same street and going to the same church for years, and yet passing each other on the street without even a friendly nod of recognition—"because they had never been introduced!" There is often too much *stiffness* even among good people. Surely worshiping together twice every Sabbath in the same church, and sitting down together at the same communion table, is a sufficient introduction. Dr. John Brown of Edinburgh, knowing this tendency, used to say to his large congregation, after reading the list of young communicants and other additions at each communion, "Now, you will consider that I have personally introduced all these to every member of this church."[1]

1. John Brown (1784–1858) was the grandson of the more famous John Brown of Haddington (1722–1787), an Edinburgh minister and professor of exegetical theology.

God sets the solitary in families, and there should be a family feeling among the members of a congregation. This feeling an elder must endeavor to promote, especially among those in his own district. Let him interest the neighbor-members in each other. They will be found willing to show each other kindness and sympathy, and thus be helps to him in his work. As a rule, none can or do help in a time of affliction like Christian neighbors.

When cholera visited Edinburgh some years ago, I found in a house (not of my district or congregation) two children who were strangers to me. On my inquiring where they came from, I got this answer from the father of the family: "Well, sir, they lived next door to us; and one night their father and mother both died of cholera, and what could my wife and I do but took the puir bairns [poor children] in beside us? I knew that our ain [own] wee things would never be the poorer for that; and we've found it so." Yes, the good man was right, for it is written, "Blessed is he that considereth the poor; the LORD will deliver him in time of trouble" (Ps. 41:1).

As akin to the subject of members being acquainted with each other, I would remark that there is too little kindness and hospitality shown to strangers at our church doors. All such should be cordially welcomed by office-bearers there, and the members should be willing at any time to give up their seats for the occasion to them. The open church door should be an echo of, "Ho, every one that thirsteth, come ye to the waters" (Isa. 55:1); "The Spirit and the Bride say, Come" (Rev. 22:17). We could mention striking and painful results of the want of such welcome; let one suffice. Many years ago now, a youth went into one of our fashionable churches. He sat down in a pew, but was soon rudely ejected by the rightful owner. He has never entered a church since that day. His pride was sorely wounded, and (in conversation with a friend, who told me) he dated his hatred of religion and the Sabbath to that act of unthinking and unchristian rudeness. Let elders, by precept and example, not be forgetful to entertain strangers at church. A casual visit to a faithful ministry has often become a day never to be forgotten.

A young elder is too apt to form hasty opinions about his people. If they have not the same spiritual history and conformation as himself, he is apt to imagine that they are not Christians at all. Inexperienced as a keeper of vineyards, he thinks that every plant that does not grow exactly to one pattern, and that his own, cannot be a living plant at all. The late Dr. Tweedie of Edinburgh once said to me, "I am more and more cautious every day of thinking or saying of any man either that he *is* or *is not* a true believer."[2] But a short experience, even of his own district, will teach an elder that there is as much diversity in the kingdom of grace as in the kingdom of nature; that the Lord brings his people in, brings them up, and brings them home in his own way, and that way sovereign and *diversified*.

An elder should get all his people to feel a deep interest in their church and congregation, in the services, meetings, classes, mission work, etc. It is always an unhealthy sign in a church member not to care much for the church and congregation he belongs to. Let people avoid getting into a grudging, grumbling way about church matters, but rather take a hearty, kindly interest in them. Many things in this world, both civil and ecclesiastical, are not what they should be and might be. But let us not be among the grumblers.

2. William Tweedie (1803–1863) was a prolific writer and served as a Free Church minister in London, Aberdeen, and Edinburgh.

Thankful for what good there is, let us put to our hand and try to make things better. Like Paul in Acts 28:3, let us gather our bundle of sticks when other people are only crying out about the cold.

You will often be asked by your people for advice as to their worldly affairs. This is natural enough, since, in many cases, the elder is the only disinterested friend a family has who is competent to give advice on such matters. This advice may be quite right to give, though *only* when particularly asked for; but we should as much as possible avoid being drawn into secular connections and complications with our church members. Of course, we shall beware of direct pecuniary responsibility, such as becoming security for rents or similar obligations. We can do much to draw a kindred together in harmony and love, yet not interfere so as to run the risk of making our good evil spoken of. Our office and our work are both spiritual, and our errand to our people is, "We seek not yours, but you" (2 Cor. 12:14).

Study Questions

1. Dickson describes a failure to "take an interest in each other" as a "great evil." What are some consequences of this evil in the life of a local church?

2. How can elders promote "a family feeling" among the members of a congregation?

3. How effectively does your church welcome visitors? What is the role of the elder in showing hospitality to strangers?

4. What practical guidelines does Dickson give elders who are asked for advice about worldly affairs? Is there anything you would add to what he says?

12

THE ELDER'S RELATIONS TO THE MINISTER AND SESSION

The elder's relations to the minister are peculiar and very important. Serving the same Master and solemnly ordained as overseers of the same flock, they should labor together affectionately and faithfully, that the Word may have free course and be glorified.

It is both our duty and our privilege to hold up our minister's hands in every way—to be intimate with him; to speak well of him; and to seek to gather up the fruits of his ministry. Let us ever welcome a call from him for help, relieving him from matters of business or routine, so as to save his time for study or pastoral work.

An elder, being accustomed in business to endless daily details, can do better, and more easily and quickly, many things that would be burdensome to a minister, whose work lies so much in continuous thought. I was struck with a remark a minister once made to me, to the effect that while he had several elders who could give him valuable help in conducting prayer meetings and giving addresses, "he was greatly in want of men who would take trouble about things."

Regular attendance at the prayer meetings is not only good for ourselves, but good also as an example to the congregation. Let us be regularly and punctually in our seats in church on Sabbath—as regularly as the minister is in the pulpit, or rather more so, for duty will sometimes call him elsewhere. The late excellent Henry Wight of Edinburgh, when absent from illness and obliged to leave all the work in the hands of his colleague, thus wrote in a letter to his congregation: "Encourage your pastor by waiting diligently on his ministry. It is inconceivable how much this enlivens and cheers a minister, but the neglecting his ministry operates as strongly in the opposite direction."[1] If this is true—as it assuredly is—as to the people, how much more is it true as to elders and other office-bearers!

Some years ago I had the privilege of visiting thirty congregations as a deputy from the General Assembly of the Free Church. What I saw and heard in the course of those visits led me to form a very deep conviction that the revival of religion and its healthy continuance depend much, under God's blessing, on the hearty cooperation of ministers and elders. It would be a kind of miracle we have no right to expect if a large harvest were gathered in when there is not loving fellowship in prayer and effort among all those who are engaged in the same field of labor.

An elder's advice may often be of use to a minister, he having a kind of experience that a minister cannot have. Our ministers are settled in congregations early in life, after spending at least eight years in study, often with few opportunities

1. The Reverend Henry Wight lived from 1801 to 1861.

of gaining experience of men and things. The wonder is not that such young ministers do occasionally make practical mistakes, but that on the whole they act so well and so wisely. It will rarely occur that judicious hints, kindly given by an elder of experience, will not be welcomed by the minister. For example, a minister once told me of the sagacious counsel he got from one of his elders at his entrance on the ministry. Among other things, the elder warned him to beware of giving heed to or sharing in the local gossip of the parish. "When this goes on in your hearing," said the elder, "not only don't join in stories against people—don't even say you disbelieve them, but say nothing at all. Perfect silence on the subject not only is the safest course for you, but is the best rebuke to gossipers, and they will soon cease to trouble you in this way." The advice was sound and judicious.

A young minister may learn much from his elders, from their local knowledge, as well as from their age and experience in the world; and they should feel it to be their duty to give him, discreetly and confidentially of course, such advice as they may think likely to be useful as to the kind of instruction most needed by the people, the style of preaching best suited to them, subjects for prayer, plans of visiting, etc. Such hints, being the results of experience, will be valued by the minister. There should, indeed, be in all matters connected with the spiritual interests of the flock a constant, confidential, and affectionate intercourse between the minister and the elders. Let them welcome and support every proposal he makes in the way of new efforts for doing good—not raising needless objections, but encouraging him in every way possible.

In no way can elders help their minister more than by warmhearted sympathy with him in his work. Every position in life has its own anxieties and cares as to health, means, family upbringing, etc.; but in addition to all these, which other men have, how heavy are the cares and burdens ever lying on the heart of a faithful minister of Christ! No business or profession has anything like them. No department of human labor ever witnessed so much self-sacrifice. The world was startled in 1843 at the sight of hundreds of ministers in Scotland surrendering their worldly all at the call of a Savior whom, having not seen, they loved (1 Peter 1:8), for when did the love of science or philosophy ever make men do such a thing?[2] But it was not the sacrifice, but the number of men who simultaneously made it, that was the novelty. All through the history of God's true church there have been instances of self-sacrifice under the cares and burdens of the ministry, the earnest seeking for the salvation of human souls in many cases wearing out the earthen vessel. John Welsh of Ayr could not sleep a whole night without prayer for the three thousand souls he felt he had to answer for, and every faithful minister feels the weight of his burden to be indeed too heavy for him.[3] With head-work and heart-work his labor is never over.

Surely it becomes a minister's people, and especially his elders, to give him their hearty sympathy and earnest prayers. Marvelous power, this power of sympathy! "Could ye not

2. Here Dickson refers to the Disruption, a major conflict within the Church of Scotland during the 1830s and early 1840s that culminated in 1843 when more than 450 ministers walked out of the General Assembly in Edinburgh to form the Free Church of Scotland. The men who formed the Free Church—to which David Dickson belonged—were evangelicals who believed that the church should be independent from any spiritual interference by the state.

3. John Welsh (1624–1681) was the grandson of John Knox. He was ordained to the ministry in 1653 but was ejected by the established church in 1662. He resorted to the fields of southwest Scotland to preach; it is recorded that in 1674 alone he preached to more than ten thousand souls.

watch with me one hour?" (Matt. 26:40). "Will ye also go away?" (John 6:67). "He took with him Peter and the two sons of Zebedee, and began to be sorrowful and very heavy" (Matt. 26:37). If the Chief Shepherd's human heart yearned for human sympathy, if his holy soul felt comforted by having his disciples beside him, is it wonderful that his servants get strength and joy also from drinking of this brook by the way?

I have said so much on this subject because of my deep conviction that we elders fall short in this duty of sympathizing fully with our ministers in their work. Scotland [and the same may be said of America] owes very much to her ministers ever since the Reformation, and she never had so many able and earnest ministers as in our own day. It is our duty to manfully show our loyalty to them, especially in these days, when so many talk flippantly and ignorantly of the minister's office and work.

In the *Memoirs* of Thomas Boston of Ettrick, he refers to one of his elders—William Biggar—who accompanied him to the sacrament at Penpont in July 1709, took ill, and died there:

Among his last words were, "Farewell, sun, moon, and stars; farewell, dear minister; and *farewell the Bible;*" which last words especially made great impression on me. He blessed God, that ever he had seen my face; which was no small comfort to me. . . . Thus the Lord pulled from me a good man, a comfortable fellow-laborer, and a supporter, or rather *the* supporter of me in my troubles in this place. He was always a friend to ministers. . . . Though he was a poor man, yet he had always a brow for a good cause, and was a faithful, useful elder; and as he was very ready to reprove sin, so he had a singular dexterity, in the matter of admonition and reproof, to speak . . . with a certain sweetness, that it was hard to take his reproofs ill. He was a most kindly, pious, good man. May the blessing of God, whose I am and whom I serve, rest on that family from generation to generation![4]

While we do not touch on what is properly the business of the church session, we may urge on our brethren the importance of regular attendance on the meetings of session. If health permits, we should attend regularly; we shall otherwise fall back in our knowledge of the business of the congregation and get out of sympathy with the work. It is depressing to the minister and to those who do attend to see few elders present, and often it causes delays that are inconvenient and may be injurious to the congregation. Meetings of session should not be held too often, nor be so protracted as to lead to family inconvenience.

Stated meetings for prayer should be held by the elders in connection with ordinary meetings for business or otherwise. In some congregations the elders meet for prayer, along with the minister, for a short time before worship. In others there is a short meeting after the afternoon service, when elders can report cases of sickness to the minister, and he can confer with them.

It tends to stimulate the elder's superintendence of his people when, at the regular meetings of session, one or two of the elders are asked to give a brief detail of their mode of visiting and of any interesting occurrences in their district. In the course of the year the session will thus hear something

4. Thomas Boston, *Memoirs,* in *The Complete Works of the Late Rev. Thomas Boston of Ettrick,* ed. Samuel M'Millan, 12 vols. (London, 1853; repr. Wheaton, Ill.: Richard Owen Roberts, 1980), 11:212.

of every district and of every elder's work. This will stimulate visitation and make the session feel that the flock is one, and some points in one elder's report may be very useful to his brethren. The minister, "as being also an elder," may sometimes give an account of his experience and methods of visiting. Where this plan has been tried, it has been found interesting and useful.

In some congregations the elders meet by themselves once a month during the winter at each other's houses, taking tea together and spending the time afterward in prayer and conference. The elder should often be in communication with the deacon of his district, advising with him as to persons requiring assistance, and aiding him as much as possible in his efforts for gathering in subscriptions for the various funds. Where there are no deacons, the elder will have to include the duties of that office with those of his own. It is to be hoped, however, that before many years elapse the scriptural office of the deacon may exist in connection with all our Presbyterian churches.

Associations of elders have lately been formed in various parts of the country. The elders of a few congregations meet together for prayer and mutual encouragement and conference as to their work. It is to be feared that, from carrying too far the spirit of ecclesiastical etiquette, villages or districts have been neglected, a congregation dreading lest they should stir up denominational jealousies if they began to work in a village where there were a few members of other churches. These things ought not to be. It would tend to much good if the elders of the various churches in each district met freely together. It would be good as well as pleasant for brethren thus to dwell and work together, and they could arrange among them for any neighboring districts that had none to care for their souls.

Study Questions

1. What are some practical ways that elders can assist their minister? Why is this kind of assistance important? How should teaching and ruling elders pray for one another?

2. In your own church, how do the gifts of your elders complement the gifts of your minister? What kind of help and assistance does your minister still need? In what ways are you assisting your minister? Are you hindering his work in any way?

3. One way in which elders assist the minister is by setting a good example for the congregation. List several practical ways to do this.

4. What are the best ways for elders to give advice to the minister? What kind of advice is it appropriate to give?

5. What are some of the special burdens that ministers carry? What does Dickson say is the most important way in which elders can help his ministry? Do you agree with his assessment? Why or why not?

6. Why is it important for elders to be faithful in attendance at public worship, prayer meetings, and meetings of session? How faithfully are the elders in your church attending to these duties?

7. List several practical ways for elders to maintain a good working partnership with deacons. How effectively are the elders and deacons working together in your church? In what specific ways does their partnership need to grow?

13

INCIDENTS — ENCOURAGEMENTS AND DISCOURAGEMENTS

Every elder who has been many years engaged in the duties of that office can recall incidents that stirred his soul at the time and have left abiding marks on his memory. It may lead to a deeper interest in the subject if I recall one or two of those that have come under my own eye. I could mention others, but I am restricted to those in which I was personally interested, and where it is impossible to awaken any painful feeling among relatives, the billows of death having, as I know, passed over all concerned.

One evening I received a message to visit one of my people, a man advanced in life, who had been subject to attacks of bronchitis. On going to his house, I found him sitting at his fireside. He held out his hand and said, "Well, I am going home at last. I have been ill before, but I know that this is my last illness. I wish you to help me to set my house in order before I die. I bless God I have not now a Savior to seek. I have some money in the bank, and I wish you to draw it out and pay the expenses of my grave and of my funeral. I have no debts, but you will pay my landlady for a month's lodging and board; and then you will use what is over to help poor old Christian people."

These were his instructions, but I hesitated to receive them, saying that I hoped he would be raised up from his present sickness. He heard me as though he heard me not, but when I spoke to him of his hope in Jesus, all seemed steady and firm. His anchor was cast within the veil, and he could say, "My Beloved is mine, and I am his" (Song 2:16). He had been for many years a steady-going Christian man, not speaking much, but very consistent and, considering his means and station in life, very liberal to the cause of God. Knowing that he had no relatives surviving, I saw it to be my duty to undertake the strange task of preparing for and paying beforehand the expenses of his funeral. I then submitted the accounts to him, and he was able to glance over them without the slightest recoil. He could face death, for to him it had lost its sting and the victory was already won. As he gave over to me the balance that remained, he said, "I am very thankful; now I have no business but with my Savior only."

My next visit found him in bed, evidently worse, and one Sabbath evening within a week of my first visit I saw he was about to depart. After my repeating to him the twenty-third psalm, he affectionately bade me "good-bye." Three hours after, he fell asleep in Jesus. I may add that a blessing seemed to rest on his loving bequest. It lasted long, like the widow's cruse of oil, and many a poor one was the better for it.

"As thy days, so shall thy strength be" (Deut. 33:25). Elders must have observed cases in which those who have been all their lifetimes subject to bondage through fear of death have had this promise fulfilled when the last enemy approached. The Lord gives dying grace for a dying hour, but he does not often give it to us when we are in full health and strength. A dear youth, who gave peculiar promise of a useful life, had been suffering from illness for a few days, when unexpectedly fatal symptoms began to show themselves. He sent for me that afternoon, and told me what had been faithfully told himself. With a mingled expression of timidity and faith he asked me as a favor to "sit beside him till he crossed the river." Only a few hours elapsed, yet how sweetly did his face brighten hour by hour! He gave me his joyful testimony that that promise was fulfilled to him: "Yea, though I walk through the valley of the shadow of death, *I will fear no evil, for thou art with me*" (Ps. 23:4). Those who have been at believers' deathbeds must have observed the fact that often there is then, as it appears to a bystander, some special discovery of the presence of Jesus, so filling the soul that there is no feeling of *leaving*, but one of *entering*—not a farewell, but a joyful welcome, reminding us of the promise to the King's bride in the forty-fifth psalm: "With gladness and rejoicing shall they be brought; they shall enter into the King's palace" (Ps. 45:15).

"The LORD will perfect that which concerneth me" (Ps. 138:8). We can sometimes observe how this is fulfilled in reference to dying believers. An aged woman who was for several years an invalid had been enabled to cast the burden of her guilt on Jesus. But she had yet one burden on her heart, the care of an only and sickly daughter. All her burdens but this she was able, she said, to cast over on him. One day when I called, her daughter said to me, "My mother is near home now, I think, for she says she has given me up to Jesus." I found it true, for she mourned over the unbelief that had led her so long to try to carry this burden herself, and she rejoiced in the thought of being in debt for everything and forever to the free grace of her covenant God. It was my last visit. She went home that night, "to be for ever with the Lord" (1 Thess. 4:17).

Elders will receive much good for their own souls in the faithful discharge of their duties. "They that wait on the LORD shall renew their strength" (Isa. 40:31). We shall not serve the Lord for naught. As Samuel Rutherford said, "They that go on errands to him for others will always get something for themselves."[1] In watering others, our own souls shall be watered. We do not serve a hard Master who prescribes a duty and sends us on the warfare at our own charges; but when duty begins privilege begins, and the promised grace begins too.

Elders will also get many a lesson as from year to year they tend their little flock. It was my privilege, when ordained as a deacon in 1844, to have in my district the well-known and beloved Alexander Paterson, the "Missionary of Kilmany."[2] Many lessons did I get from that "old disciple," now long since gone to his rest and reward.

"Every life has its lesson" is a remark especially true of every believer. For the last thirty years I have kept a list of the names of all friends who have departed. That is now a very long list, and there are in it many names of the "just made perfect" (Heb. 12:23). I am struck with observing that

---

1. Samuel Rutherford (1600–1661) was one of Scotland's greatest theologians and political theorists. His most influential writing was *Lex, Rex* (1644), a treatise that challenged the divine right of kings and asserted that people must consent to their royal powers. At the same time, Rutherford believed that citizens had a God-given right to resist tyranny. His devotional writings remain valuable for the church, especially his *Letters* (1664), which have frequently been reprinted.

2. Alexander Paterson (1790–1851) was minister in Kilmany, Scotland.

in reference to most of these, there is a useful lesson left on my memory. So will every elder find in reference to his people. Each individual believer will be on his mind as a living lesson of some grace of the Spirit. How many testimonies to God's love and faithfulness will be furnished even by the small section of the vineyard of which he is the overseer! The work of the eldership will be in this and many other ways its own reward.

We should also here add the remark that, while each elder should have not only a definite purpose, but also a definite plan of operation, yet it is of great importance, for both his own sake and that of his people, that he should, in his way of carrying out his plans, be ever ready to avail himself of new suggestions. Occasional variety in matters of detail gives a new freshness and interest that help to prevent the feeling of dullness and formality. We must avoid, on the one hand, constant change of plans and, on the other hand, unvarying routine. The working of our plans should have the benefit of our growing practical experience.

Humbled for past unworthiness, let elders work on steadily and prayerfully, looking for and *expecting* the blessing. There will be fruit of our sowing, for that is promised; and usually we shall see fruit, though that is not promised. Some men have passed away from their work to their reward thinking that they had been of little or no use in the world, when it was found that much good had been done by them. With others, again, there is a tendency to exaggerate in their own minds what they have been enabled to do. While it is very encouraging to know that the Lord has blessed our work, it requires much grace for ourselves to safely see much fruit. Everyone is not led to say, or at least to *feel,* as Dr.

Chalmers did when told of a conversion under his preaching, "That is very humbling."[3]

Then we are apt to forget a great principle of God's Word: "One soweth and another reapeth" (John 4:37). In the rescue of a drowning man, one person might give the alarm, a second might bring a rope, a third might throw it to him, and a fourth might draw him to shore. It could be said truly of all these four that they were instruments in saving the man from death. So it is in the salvation of souls, as proved by the history of individuals. God works all in all, but he often uses several different instruments for the ingathering of his elect, "that no flesh should glory in his presence" (1 Cor. 1:29). How often would our poor hearts try to get credit for being the *only* instrument in the salvation of a sinner! No, we can be of much use, and I believe often are of much use, where we see no necessary connection between our own work and the salvation of men. It is, in one sense, a humbling view. It excludes all boasting in ourselves. It is well for many that the good they do is hidden from them till they are able to bear it. And yet it is very encouraging too, for though we may not be able to do any great thing, we can yet do many little things. Let us rejoice to be even the smallest and humblest link in that chain of love and grace by which Jesus is drawing sinners to himself. How well for us and the souls we care for that, from first to last, "salvation is of the LORD" (Jonah 2:9)!

Elders, like all other laborers in the vineyard, have much need to go softly and to watch and pray. Self-seeking and men-pleasing are too apt to come in and blunt the edge of our motives and actions. The enemy is often allowed to make

---

3. For more on Thomas Chalmers, see page 45.

much use of God's own people in doing his work of evil. The praise of good men is in some respects more insidious and dangerous than that of others. Scriptural commendation is not flattery, but there are good people in the world who do much harm by ill-timed and unnecessary commendation, which may spread as mildew over the souls of those they commend so much. If it is true that "flattery is sweet, even from the lips of an idiot," how much sweeter will it be, and how much more dangerous, to the poor, half-sanctified human heart, coming from "such good people"! Avoid people who are always telling you, directly or indirectly, what a good man you are and what a great deal of good you do.

Let us honor the Holy Spirit. We are entirely dependent on him. The more we feel this as churches, as congregations, as pastors, as elders, the more we will say, "All our springs are in thee" (Ps. 87:7). We cannot continue to exist as churches unless he adds to the churches daily such as shall be saved (Acts 2:47), and gives his added people to know the privilege expressed in the words, "Freely ye have received, *freely give*" (Matt. 10:8). We cannot live on the memory of past blessing; we must be daily pleading, "Wilt thou not revive us again, that thy people may rejoice in thee?" (Ps. 85:6).

As elders, individually set to watch over the people committed to us, let us feel that we can do real, lasting good to the souls of our people only so far as the Spirit blesses, and no further. And this blessing is sure, for he is faithful that has promised (Heb. 10:23): "If ye then, being evil, know how to give good gifts unto your children, *how much more* will your heavenly Father give the Holy Spirit to them that ask him" (Luke 11:13)!

Elders will meet with discouragements. In some of the members and adherents there may seem to be little to give us hope that our prayers have been answered. Some who ran well are hindered (Gal. 5:7). In others the cares of the world and the deceitfulness of riches appear to choke the Word (Matt. 13:22), and we may attend deathbeds that want the full assurance of an abundant entrance into the kingdom. But our chief discouragement will come from our own hearts—from our coldness, our unbelief, our lukewarmness, our tendency to get into a formal routine.

Let us "encourage ourselves in the LORD our God" (1 Sam. 30:6)—in his sure word of promise and his evident answers to prayer. We feel persuaded that in no similar work for Christ—not even in Sabbath-school teaching—are men more encouraged to sow beside all waters than in the duties of the eldership. To be but hewers of wood and drawers of water in such a Master's house would be a great honor, but ours is still greater. As "friends of the Bridegroom" (John 3:29), to be helps and witnesses to the betrothal of sinners to Jesus; to stand by and see the salvation of God; to watch the operations of his hand; to guide and encourage his ransomed ones on their way Zionward; and to see many of them safe home before himself—this is the privilege of a faithful elder.

It is but a few short years any of us will have to do this service for our Lord here below. Let us do it heartily, with all our might, and always as to the Lord. "And when the Chief Shepherd shall appear, ye shall receive a crown of glory that fadeth not away" (1 Peter 5:4).

Study Questions

1. What are the most life-changing experiences you have had in your work as an elder or in other Christian work? Identify several of the most memorable people you have served. What have you learned from them?

2. What duty does an elder have to those who are dying?

3. List several rewards and blessings that God has promised to elders who are faithful in their work.

4. Elders need to have "a definite plan of operation." They also need to be willing to adjust their plans as the situation changes, and as they grow in their understanding of their office. After reading *The Elder and His Work,* what do you identify as the most important changes you need to make in your own plan for ministry?

5. Dickson warns against "self-seeking" and "men-pleasing." Describe how you face these temptations in your own life and ministry.

6. What is the role of the Holy Spirit in the ministry of the elder?

7. What discouragements do elders commonly face in their work? Which of these discouragements have you faced? What are an elder's greatest sources of encouragement?

David Dickson was an ordained elder in nineteenth-century Scotland. At age thirty he was ordained as an elder in the Free New North Church, and he served as clerk of session for thirty-three years. His practical experiences as an elder led him to publish *The Elder and His Work*.

George Kennedy McFarland (Ph.D., Bryn Mawr College) has been an elder for more than twenty-five years at Tenth Presbyterian Church in Philadelphia. He is dean of the faculty and history teacher at Delaware County Christian School.

Philip G. Ryken (D.Phil., Oxford University) is senior minister of Tenth Presbyterian Church, Philadelphia. He has written fourteen books and edited three. Among the former are *City on a Hill: Reclaiming the Biblical Pattern for the Church in the 21st Century* (2003). Among the latter are *The Communion of Saints: Living in Fellowship with the People of God* (2001). He also coedited *Give Praise to God: A Vision for Reforming Worship: Celebrating the Legacy of James Montgomery Boice* (2003).